5-MINUTE MINDFULNESS MEDITATIONS FOR TEENS

5-MINUTE

MINDFULNESS MEDITATIONS

FOR TEENS

NICOLE LIBIN, Ph.D.

ROCKRIDGE
PRESS

Interior and Cover Designer: Emma Hall
Photo Art Director/Art Manager: Michael Hardgrove
Editor: Justin Hartung
Production Editor: Kurt Shulenberger
All graphics used under license from Shutterstock.com

ISBN: Print 978-1-64152-837-5 | eBook 978-1-64152-838-2

R0

For my mommelah.
For everything.

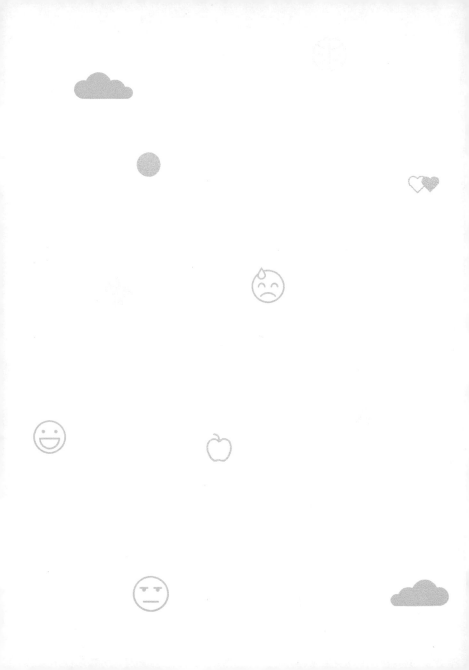

Contents

Introduction

Being a human is hard.

Being a teenager might just be the hardest part of all.

You're often treated like a child but are expected to behave like an adult.

You're asked to make decisions that will impact the rest of your life without being totally clear on what you want, what feels right, or what's out there.

You're figuring out where you fit and who you are, which can make you feel like there's something wrong with you, especially when you just aren't sure of either.

You love your friends, but there's so much drama.

You love your family, but sometimes it feels like you live on completely different planets.

You're trying to more fully understand your sexual and gender identity and be true to yourself while living up to parental and societal expectations.

You want to feel comfortable in your own skin, but everywhere you turn, you get messages telling you that you should look or be some other way—messages about how or why you don't measure up.

And because it's all new and it's all challenging, what worked before to help you manage stress and deal with your life can seem totally inadequate now. No wonder teens are more stressed than ever before and are actually the most stressed generation in America right now.

The practices in this book offer freedom. They give you the tools to train your brain, so you can choose who and how you are, instead of being pushed around, either by the outside world or by your own unwanted emotions and thoughts. And all you need is you.

I don't think it's too blunt to say that I wasn't a happy teenager. I was lucky to be raised in a loving home with parents who supported me. And yet, what I mostly remember is being hypersensitive and feeling like I didn't fit in anywhere. I wasn't a kid and I wasn't an adult, and being in between felt like the worst of both worlds. I've always been exceptionally hard on myself, feeling like I could never be good enough. I felt like my body was wrong, and I constantly compared myself to other people. My life on the outside was good, and I know that I was, and still am, privileged. But on the inside, I just felt wrong. Of course, it wasn't all bad—but, as I think back, the bad definitely outweighs the good in my mind.

I remember visiting various doctors, therapists, and teachers and feeling like they saw me as a problem they were supposed to solve. And that also felt wrong. I didn't need to be fixed. What I really needed was for someone to give me some tools so I could help myself and be the one in charge, rather than feeling like I was at the mercy of my restless brain or the rest of the world. I needed tools to help me be okay with being me—and maybe even like myself more along the way.

Sadly, mindfulness didn't become mainstream until long after my teenage years. But, although it took more time to reach me, mindfulness is that set of tools for me. It doesn't make all my problems go away. I still get depressed. I still sometimes think my legs should look different, or I look at other people and think they're doing better than I am. I still have a voice in my head that tells me I'm not good enough. What mindfulness does is help me choose how much attention I give to that voice. It lets me hear it without beating myself up, and then it helps me turn the volume down. Jon Kabat-Zinn, the founder of the modern mindfulness movement, once said, "You can't stop the waves, but you can learn to surf." The quick-and-easy five-minute meditations in this book will provide you with the tools to ride the sometimes amazing, often challenging waves of being a teenager.

CHAPTER ONE

What Does Mindfulness Meditation Even Mean?

If you do an image search for meditation, you'll probably see some version of the same picture: a (conventionally) super-attractive person sitting in a twisted yoga posture, probably on the beach, looking calm and peaceful and kind of perfect. If you've ever actually tried to meditate, chances are you didn't feel calm, peaceful, or perfect. Maybe the only thing you felt was restless or sleepy; maybe the only thing you noticed was that your brain never shuts up.

The good news is that you don't need to be calm, peaceful, or perfect to meditate. You don't have to be anything other than who and how you are. Meditation is really just a workout for your mind; it's a way of purposefully training your mind to be however you want it to be in any given moment. And mindfulness is all about being with what's happening in the present moment—seeing it and allowing it to be just as it is, right now.

While it's important to recognize that mindfulness meditation has its roots in Buddhism, the practices and ideas shared here can be used by anyone from any background or religious tradition.

How to Practice Mindfulness

Plot twist: You actually already know how to be mindful! While you read this sentence, notice your awareness of the following: the meaning of the words, the sounds you hear around you, the thoughts in your head, and the rhythm of your breathing. Congratulations—you just practiced mindfulness! Mindfulness meditation just means doing this deliberately.

To break it down further, mindfulness is the practice of paying attention to what's happening right now in your mind and body in a kind, interested, and nonjudgmental way. It allows you to be aware of what's happening as it happens, rather than getting caught up in stories, judgments, or worries about what did, might, could, or should be happening. Once you have that awareness, you can respond to what's going on in a way that you choose rather than reacting on autopilot. Mindfulness trains you to focus on what you want when you want and to ground your attention in your body and senses, so you don't get carried away with thoughts and emotions (if you don't want to).

It's all about that feeling when you want to give up, because your brain is telling you that you're too ugly, too fat, too dumb, or too skinny; when you can't sleep at night because your mind will not settle down; when you actually did something great but feel like you don't deserve any praise or love; or when you start to freak out because someone didn't message you back. If you've experienced those or similar feelings, you know how your automatic reactions aren't always helpful. Mindfulness lets you train your mind to see what's happening in a way that's appreciative rather than judgmental, and accepting rather than resistant or analytical. That perspective lets you be kinder to yourself as you look in the mirror, get more rest because you can let go of worries more easily, feel the pride of your accomplishments or enjoy the love you deserve, and be more patient with yourself and others when you aren't getting the response you wanted.

At its best, your mind is amazing. It lets you learn, solve problems, play sports, try new things, and more. At its worst, your mind can be like an Internet troll—judgmental, mean, quick to argue, and UNRELENT-INGLY LOUD. It can also be like an overzealous therapist, analyzing every little thing you do, obsessing about the past or what's coming next or why things ended up this way. Mindfulness is like a friend, teacher, or parent who tells you that you're doing great, this too shall pass, and you don't have to listen to that shouting jerk or the nattering worrier. Mindfulness trains you to be here now, just as you are, and know that that's okay. As cheesy as it sounds, it's about being a friend to yourself and your experiences rather than needing to change them, get rid of them, or believe the voice that says you're not good enough.

How It Can Help You

This is not about "fixing" yourself or getting rid of who you are. It's about relating to yourself and the world around you in a way that promotes your own happiness and well-being. It doesn't mean that life will suddenly be perfect, but rather that you can be kinder to yourself when everything feels wrong. It's actually really empowering, because you get to be in charge of your mind rather than it being in charge of you.

Sadly, the superpowers of mindfulness are limited. It won't make exams, curfews, demanding bosses, mean people, or unrealistic body standards go away. It can't do much about racism, homophobia, or sexism on a broad scale. But it can help you deal with all of that in a way that makes your life easier, letting you find more compassion for yourself and other people. Instead of hating the exam, calling yourself dumb, or being sure you're going to fail, mindfulness lets you just *take* the exam. It lets you see what's happening for what it is (nerves, mistakes, pain, discomfort, frustration, distracting thoughts) without adding extra stress. The goal isn't to make those pains or discomforts go away (which is usually out of your control, anyway), but to see that they are actually just uncomfortable feelings that won't last forever. You might still be stressed, but you won't be stressed out.

You can't change a lot of what happens to you. You can't change the past, mistakes you've made, much of what you look like, where you're born, etc. But, if you can see and acknowledge those experiences, then you can decide how you want to relate to them. With practice, you can live your life in a way that lets you accept what you can't change and have the strength and compassion to be the person you want to be.

Neuroscientists are discovering more and more about how our brains can grow and change based on our experiences and habits. Basically, your brain gets good at what it practices. This concept, called neuroplasticity, is what meditation is all about. You probably weren't very good the first time you picked up a violin, hopped on a skateboard, or attempted a three-pointer—but the more you practiced, the better you got. Your brain works the same way. The more you engage in self-criticism, catastrophizing, and judging yourself and others, the better you'll become at those reactions; they'll become more automatic and will be easier to access whether you like them or not. The good news is that every time you pause before reacting, take a breath, are kind to yourself, focus on your good qualities more than the bad, or forgive yourself for making a mistake, the more those habits will become a part of who you are. By reading this book and completing these exercises, you are choosing how you will train your brain and what kind of person you will be.

Need More Convincing?

Studies show that mindfulness meditation helps teens improve:

OVERALL MENTAL HEALTH AND WELL-BEING. You'll feel less stress, more self-compassion, and less self-criticism.

FOCUS AND ATTENTION. You can focus on what you want, when you want.

WORKING MEMORY. You can actually remember what you're studying in class.

EMPATHY. You can feel more connected to other people and less isolated.

ACADEMIC PERFORMANCE. You'll do better in school with more focus and less stress.

RESILIENCE. You can handle the roller coaster of life more skillfully.

SELF-ESTEEM AND SELF-REGULATION. You'll feel better about yourself and be less likely to lose it when things go sideways.

EMOTIONAL REGULATION. You get more of a say in how you feel.

QUALITY OF SLEEP. You can let your mind rest, so you will, too.

TEST PERFORMANCE. You can boost your working memory and reduce mind wandering.

And mindful teens show a decrease in:

- » Stress
- » Depressive symptoms
- » General anxiety
- » Test anxiety

Famous People Who Meditate

Sometimes it helps to know that you aren't alone in trying out this whole mindfulness thing. Famous people from many different fields do this practice:

ATHLETES
- LeBron James
- Derek Jeter
- Misty May-Treanor
- Ricky Williams
- Kerri Walsh Jennings

ACTORS
- Hugh Jackman
- Keanu Reeves
- Danai Gurira
- Chloë Grace Moretz

MUSICIANS
- Katy Perry
- Big Sean
- Kendrick Lamar
- Lady Gaga

Reading about mindfulness is like reading about music—you can't get the full experience only through books. To get what mindfulness is all about, you have to try it.

This book offers a series of foundational meditations in chapter 2. These can be applied to almost every part of your life. They cover everything from using your breathing to focus your attention, to dealing with emotions and thoughts skillfully, to cultivating gratitude and self-compassion. The rest of the book addresses specific scenarios. Each practice includes one of four tips:

- **BUDDY UP:** how to do the practice with a friend, family member, or partner
- **CHANGE IT UP:** ways to vary the practice
- **TAKE IT FURTHER:** how to dive deeper and explore the practice further
- **AM I DOING THIS RIGHT?:** helpful hints and suggestions, or common obstacles

RESPONDING VS. REACTING AND EXPECTATIONS VS. INTENTIONS

These meditations build the basic skills for mindfulness. You're training yourself to respond rather than react. Mindfulness teacher Sam Himelstein describes the difference: "Responding is when you think before you act. Reacting is when you act before you think."

When I started meditating, I noticed that I had lots of automatic reactions about meditation itself. It was a combination of "this is amazing, it's going to solve all my problems," "this is a huge waste of time," and "why am I the only one who can't do it?"—none of which was all that helpful for simply being in the present moment.

The ability to respond rather than react can have life-changing, real-world implications. I've worked with teens who use these tools to stay focused while being taunted by competitors at major sporting competitions. Others were able to walk away from a fight rather than get sucked in. One student told me about a time she was able to pause and change her mind before hurting herself. In a society where you're judged and targeted for things you can't control, like your sexuality, the color of your skin, or your body or gender identity, being able to choose how you respond can be the difference between well-being and stress—or even safety and danger.

Having said that, it's important to let go of expectations. Of course, you wouldn't be reading this book if you didn't want to get something from it. But the somewhat annoying and totally paradoxical thing about meditation is that the more expectations you have and the more you try to make something happen, the less likely it is to happen.

It's like when you tell yourself to calm down or someone tells you, "Cheer up, stop being so stressed." Does it work? Almost never. The best way to actually calm down or stop stressing is to respond rather than react, to have intentions rather than expectations. Instead of fighting the stress or expecting to feel something different, you can acknowledge it with kindness. The stress might not go away, but you aren't beating yourself up for something you can't control or getting mad because it doesn't fit with how your brain thinks things should be. The best way to approach meditation is to be with what's happening rather than trying to get somewhere else.

7 KEY THINGS TO REMEMBER

1. **YOU CAN'T DO IT WRONG.** The whole point is to notice what's happening as it's happening. Even if the thing you notice is the thought "this is stupid," that still counts.

2. **IF YOU THINK OF IT AS HOMEWORK, IT FEELS AS CRAPPY AS HOMEWORK.** Try to think of it as a break or a rest instead. It's a time to chill out rather than another thing to do or get right.

3. **THE GOAL IS NOT TO MAKE EVERYTHING HAPPY OR CALM.** That means that whatever you feel is okay. Mindfulness isn't about making yourself feel any particular way, and it's not about stopping how you currently are. It's just seeing (and hearing, smelling, tasting, touching, thinking, and feeling) what's happening as it happens.

4. **MINDFULNESS ISN'T ASKING YOU TO SIT BACK AND LET THE WORLD WALK ALL OVER YOU.** If you want to change something, you still get to change it. Ultimately, you can't change anything without seeing it first. Mindfulness helps you do that.

5. **YOU DEFINITELY WON'T STOP THINKING WHEN YOU MEDITATE!** It's not about making your mind go blank or getting rid of thoughts. It's just noticing what's happening and choosing how much and what kind of attention to give it. Everyone's mind wanders.

6. **IF YOU EVER FEEL OVERWHELMED BY WHAT YOU EXPERIENCE WHILE MEDITATING (OR OTHERWISE), TRY TO REMEMBER THAT EVEN IF IT FEELS SCARY OR REALLY INTENSE, YOU ARE OKAY.** You aren't doing it wrong (meditation, or just living in general). If you do get overwhelmed, you might want to open your eyes if they're closed, take a few deep breaths, and use your senses to connect to your environment. (See pages 28 and 132 for more.)

7. **PEOPLE CALL IT THE *PRACTICE* OF MINDFULNESS OR MEDITATION FOR A REASON.** Like any skill, it takes practice. If it feels weird or awkward at first, don't worry. The more you do it, the more natural it becomes.

Tips for Success

Mindfulness is actually easy. The challenge is remembering to do it. Use these tips as a way to support the habit you are trying to build.

POSTURE MATTERS. You can meditate in any posture that feels comfortable. It can help to sit with a straight spine, a bit more upright and energized than you normally would. This posture is probably different from how you usually sit, and it can promote clarity and concentration. It's better to practice on a straight-backed chair or on a cushion on the floor rather than on a couch or in bed (you're less likely to fall asleep). Your eyes can be either closed or open with a soft gaze such that you aren't really looking at anything (unless you are doing a practice that asks you to look around your environment).

MAKE IT A HABIT. The best way to make mindfulness, compassion, and nonjudgment a more permanent part of who you are is to practice regularly. Try to find a regular time when you can practice these meditations (maybe between school and work, between classes, or right before bedtime). At the same time, experiment with practicing informally throughout your day. Anytime you can stop and take a breath is an opportunity to train your brain.

USE A TIMER. It's really helpful to choose how long you will meditate for and set a timer (it can even be your phone) for that length of time in advance. Then hide the timer behind you, so you won't be tempted to peek at it. There are lots of free timer apps you can use.

KEEP A JOURNAL. A meditation journal is another helpful tool. It can be a fancy notebook or just notes on your phone. Make it as detailed or as brief as you like—for example, "Practiced for five minutes, noticed my mind felt crazy and felt my breath in my nose." The journal helps support the habit and keeps you accountable.

FIND SUPPORT. Having a friend who knows what you're doing and who can support you is one of the best ways to promote a regular mindfulness practice. You might text each other once a day with a brief reminder like "Breathe" or "Pause," to share what you noticed when you meditated, or even just send a thumbs-up emoji after you've practiced. Some people really like meditating with others; others prefer to do it alone. Do what works for you.

Also, while this book is a great way to start your mindfulness journey, it's especially helpful to have someone who can guide you in your practice. There are lots of free resources online, including guided meditations. Check out the resources at the end of the book and/or look up teachers or meditation groups in your area. Lots of teachers offer stuff online, too.

DON'T GIVE UP. Some of the meditations will feel like a great fit for you. Others might not. For example, if you have asthma or experience anxiety, paying attention to your breath might be unhelpful. Try to trust yourself, but also don't give up too easily. If it feels challenging, that's totally normal. If it feels overwhelming or painful, trust yourself and choose a different practice or take a break and come back when it feels right.

YOU KNOW YOURSELF BEST. Ask yourself what you need to do to make this commitment or to bring yourself back when you lose track. Maybe you need to set reminders on your phone or download an app for this. Maybe you need to write a note for your mirror or schedule it into your calendar. It's like exercise—sometimes you know you should do it even if you don't feel like it. Once you start, chances are you'll keep going.

What You Shouldn't Expect from Meditation

First, although meditation can have lots of benefits, there are some things it just can't do. For better or for worse, your meditation practice can't change someone else's behavior. And although meditation can be highly beneficial for more serious mental challenges like depression and anxiety, it isn't the only answer and can sometimes be difficult to do if you are in the throes of a severe episode. Remember that you aren't alone. Talk to a parent or counselor if you need help.

Second, mindfulness is all about being with what's happening in a way that's kind and nonjudgmental. But that doesn't mean you have to accept everything that happens to you. You still get to trust yourself and your judgment and reject anything that hurts you. If a person is doing something to you that you think is wrong, is hurting you, or just feels bad, please tell someone. Tell a friend, parent, or teacher. Call a distress number (these are really easy to find with a quick Internet search). Mindfulness is about being with the things that we can be with; it's not about putting up with something that's totally unacceptable.

CHAPTER TWO

Foundational Meditations

> *It's not what you look at that matters,*
> *it's what you see.*
> **HENRY DAVID THOREAU**

The practices in this chapter serve as the basic skills for your mindfulness exploration. You are training awareness of this moment and nonjudgment of what's happening. Subsequent chapters will build on these foundations, and the exercises will always come back to being with this moment just as it is, with kindness and curiosity.

While it sounds like it's all about the mind or brain, mindfulness is really about putting your attention in your body. Research shows that people with more body awareness are less prone to stress. The practices here will guide you to ground your awareness in your body as it is and use your senses to notice what's happening as if you're experiencing it for the very first time. Whenever your mind wanders or is judging, you get to notice it and gently bring your attention back to what you're feeling and sensing in this moment.

Finding Your Breath

When your mind is racing, your heart is pounding, or you feel out of control or stressed out, focusing on the feeling of your breath can help you let go of things you can't control right now, bringing you back to the present moment. It's like a reset button for your mind.

1. Find a posture that feels comfortable.

2. Take a few deep breaths. Notice how that feels.

3. Allow your breathing to return to whatever feels natural.

4. Take a few moments to become aware of any obvious areas of tension in your body and then consciously relax them.

5. Find the spot in your body where your breath feels the most obvious to you. You can even place your hand on that spot to feel more connected.

6. Placing all of your attention on your breathing, notice what it feels like, in your body, to breathe. It's not thinking about or picturing breathing, but rather feeling the physical sensations. You don't have to make your breath special or deep. Just notice how it feels as it is, as if you've never felt it before.

7. Notice everything you can about the physical feeling of breathing. Is it fast? Slow? Deep? Shallow? Smooth? Choppy? Notice how it moves or shifts.

8. When your mind wanders (which it definitely will!), take a moment to notice where it's gone. A wandering mind isn't a mistake; it's just another thing to notice in the present moment. Then gently bring your attention back to the feeling of breathing.

9. You can use a soft mental label throughout this (or any) practice. In your mind, say words like "in, out" or "rising, falling" to accompany the action. When your mind wanders, you can label categories (for example, "planning" or "worrying").

10. When you're done, take a few more deep breaths and notice how you feel.

CHANGE IT UP

While this practice is perfect for a formal meditation, it's also easy to do throughout your day. Any time you notice the feeling of breathing, you are bringing yourself back to the present moment and training your mind to be more aware, patient, and focused. Whenever you need a reset or rest, see if you can take a breath or two.

Being Present in Your Body

Like the breath, your body is your ally in meditation. It helps you let go of thoughts running through your mind and anchors you to this moment. In fact, it's useful to think of your body and breath as an anchor. The mind takes you away from the present moment, but once you see that you've gone somewhere else, you can focus on your body and breath to bring you back to right here and right now.

1. Find a comfortable, upright posture. Close your eyes or assume a soft gaze.

2. Take a few deep breaths. Notice how you feel.

3. Let your breathing return to whatever feels natural right now.

4. Take a moment to set your intention to be with your body and let go of the focus on thinking for now. Think of this as a break from the constant busyness of your mind.

5. See if you can be really curious about, even fascinated by this body you inhabit. Isn't it amazing that you have a body that works at all?

6. You can focus on your body as a whole or just two or three spots to be your anchor. Check out what it feels like to have a body. What can you feel? Heaviness? Lightness? Tingling? Warmth? Itchiness? Pressure?

7. Whenever your mind wanders, remember that your body is your anchor. Acknowledge that thoughts have taken over. Then come back to the feelings in your body without judging yourself.

8. Notice that your body is always changing and that emotions are felt as physical sensations. Check out how anxiety, jitteriness, calm, fatigue, happiness, boredom, etc. feel in your body.

9. When you're finished, take a few deep breaths. Remember that you can always come back to this anchor for a full meditation or just a one-second check-in.

CHANGE IT UP

Notice how your body feels not only while sitting in meditation or at rest, but also when active. Observe how your legs move when you're playing sports or how your arm holds the bow of your violin. Explore your body posture when you're texting, and just for a second, see how it makes you feel. Sometimes relaxing the body can relax the mind and vice versa.

Body Scan

Body scans are helpful and grounding, especially when you feel out of control. They can be a good way to let go of tension when you come home from school or before bedtime. The goal is to move your attention up your body, feeling any and all sensations in a kind, curious way, without trying to make anything happen or judging what's there. If you feel uncomfortable, try to just notice what that feels like without needing to move or change it.

1. Sit or lie comfortably. Close your eyes if that feels okay. Notice what it feels like to be you right now.

2. Take a few deep breaths and see how your breathing feels in your body.

3. Let your breathing return to normal.

4. Starting at your feet, explore anything you can feel. You might notice tingling, pressure, warmth, coolness, tension, heaviness, lightness, vibration, and more. Notice any contact with furniture or clothing. Check out what you can feel, what you can't, and how it changes as you observe it.

5. Let go of the focus on your feet.

6. Next bring awareness to any sensations in your legs. What can you notice?

7. Move your attention to your back and butt. Do you feel pressure? Tingling? Warmth?

8. Exploring your stomach and chest, can you feel your breath going in and out? Can you sense your heart beating?

9. Turn your attention to your shoulders, arms, and hands. What do you feel here? Can you feel the air on your skin? Any tingling, heat, or tension?

10. Moving to the neck, face, and head, explore each area as if you've never felt them before. Can you feel your teeth and nose? What do lips or cheekbones actually feel like?

11. Finish by noticing feelings at the top of your head, then take a moment to notice your whole body sitting or lying there.

12. If you have time, try exploring each foot individually, then each ankle, calf, knee, and so on.

TAKE IT FURTHER

We all have pretty complicated relationships with our bodies. Use the body scan to recognize what thoughts or judgments automatically come up and see if you can call them what they are—just judgments or habits, not necessarily the truth. All you really have are those physical sensations in any given moment.

Be Here Now

Sometimes, you feel like life is moving too fast, every-thing's wrong, or your brain is too full—that feeling when you want the world to stop, so you can pause for a minute.

Teddy Roosevelt said, "Comparison is the thief of joy." The more you focus on what's wrong in this moment, what you might be missing (also known as FOMO—Fear of Missing Out), or what others have that you don't, the harder it is to access the joy—or even the "okayness"—available in any moment. That doesn't mean you have to passively accept everything that happens. And it doesn't mean you can't strive or want more. It just means seeing when striving is helpful and when it gets in the way. In this meditation, use your senses to bring yourself back to the present, enjoying this moment as it is. Because, if you think about it, this moment is really the only one you have.

1. Find a comfortable posture. Notice how your body feels, paying particular attention to your feet on the ground or your body against the furniture or floor.

2. Take a few deep breaths. Explore how that feels.

3. Next, let your breath be natural. Feel yourself breathing for a bit.

4. Focus on your senses. With as much interest and curiosity as possible, check out everything your senses are telling you right now. Imagine you were asked to write a story or draw a picture about everything you experience.

5. Notice what your eyes see. Check out color, texture, light, movement, shadows. What is it like to see? Is there anything noteworthy or different?

6. Now notice hearing. Imagine that the sounds are notes in your favorite song. Notice when the song is loud or soft, harsh or soothing. Check out tapping, rhythm, even the sound of silence.

7. Continue the exploration with touch (contact, pressure, temperature, vibration, movement), smell (obvious, subtle, powerful, pleasant, familiar, unfamiliar, sour), and taste (bitter, salty, sweet, lingering, spicy).

8. This isn't about figuring out what you're sensing. Rather, it's about noticing the senses and experiences themselves and being as captivated as possible.

9. You might find just one thing in this moment to rest your attention on and appreciate, letting your senses rest on that thing just one more time.

10. Finally, come back to the feeling of your body in this moment. Take a few more deep breaths.

CHANGE IT UP

If you feel really overwhelmed or out of control, a "five-four-three-two-one" countdown version of this meditation can be helpful. Look for five things you see, four things you hear, three things you can feel or are touching, two things you smell (or recall smells you enjoy), and one thing you can taste (or recall a taste you enjoy). It gives your mind something to do and calms your nervous system.

Your Happy/Safe Place Visualization

Sometimes, you just need to take a break in a place where you feel safe and relaxed, even if you can't actually go anywhere. This visualization practice is all about that happy and safe place.

1. Find a place where you can relax for a few minutes, somewhere you won't be disturbed and can really let go. Make sure your phone is turned off.

2. Take a few deep breaths wherever you are. Notice how it feels to pause and breathe for just a moment.

3. Come back to breathing normally.

4. Take a moment to set an intention. Something like, "This time is a break. I am giving myself a chance to rest." Remind yourself that this is an important part of self-care and that it's even necessary to reset your current state of mind.

5. Bring to mind a place where you can feel peaceful, contented, and at ease. It could be a place you've been or somewhere you imagine. It might be resting in a hammock on a beach, floating on a raft on a river, or even lying on a cloud. It doesn't have to make sense. It just has to be someplace that fits for you right now.

CONTINUED

6. Picture yourself in this place. Use all of your senses to bring this place to mind in as much detail as possible. For example, if you pictured a beach, imagine the wind on your face, the smell of salt water, or the sound of lapping waves.

7. Let your body and your mind feel totally supported. You don't have to do anything. If you notice any areas of tension, try to relax them.

8. Notice what it feels like to be in this place. Really give yourself permission to be here, for these moments.

9. As you finish, take a few deep breaths. Imagine that these breaths can bring you back to this safe place at any time, whenever you need it.

AM I DOING THIS RIGHT?

Although visualization is a lovely tool, it tends to promote escaping from the present moment, whereas mindfulness is all about acknowledging what's happening with a kind heart. Use this practice when you really need a break. Once you've done this meditation, go back to the breath or body meditations and notice that you can create that quiet, safe space inside you, just by being with your breathing.

Soaking in the Good

This practice is about connecting to what's positive in the present, no matter what else is happening. You're choosing to see the good and really savor it. The more you focus on what's good, joyful, and kind, the more you'll notice, remember, and see it in the future. Use this practice anytime something pleasant is going on or as your go-to meditation if you often feel overwhelmed or it feels impossible to concentrate.

1. Start by pausing and taking a few deep breaths. Notice how you feel.

2. Let your breathing be natural. Explore what your body feels like.

3. Turn your attention toward something that makes you happy or at ease. If you're meditating, bring something good to mind or look around for something pleasant that you can see. You can also focus on the good as it happens. When you're laughing with your friends or walking outside, tune in to pleasant feelings. When someone compliments you, instead of dismissing it or moving on to the next thing, make a deliberate effort to feel those good feelings you earned.

CONTINUED

4. If you can't think of anything good, that's totally normal. Just use your senses to find something pleasant that you see or feel and explore that.

5. Notice how this feels in your body. What is it like to be with something that feels genuinely good? Can you connect to it with all of your senses?

6. In your mind or aloud, say a word or two that connects to this good feeling. How does this feel or what do you notice primarily? (Soft, pleasing, gentle, light, etc.)

7. Then allow yourself to really linger on and notice that quality. Keep coming back to the soft, pleasing, or gentle quality.

8. Now imagine you could make this a permanent part of you, like you could absorb it through your skin. Really soak it in.

9. See how long you can make this feeling last.

10. When you're done, notice how you feel now.

AM I DOING THIS RIGHT?

If you ever struggle with or feel overwhelmed by practices that turn inward (focusing on breath, emotions, or your body), this is the practice for you. Use your senses to find anything in your environment that catches your eye or feels pleasant, okay, or beautiful. It helps to be outside or by a window, so you can connect with nature. Let your attention rest on and try to soak in that pleasant feeling. You can do this instead of any other meditation. It's just as powerful and helps you reconnect to feelings of well-being, which might not be so accessible all the time.

Sending Kind Thoughts

One way to change your relationship to yourself and others, and to build your capacity for kindness, is to nurture thoughts and qualities that promote your well-being. The idea here is to soothe the nervous system by connecting to kind wishes for yourself and others.

1. Find a comfortable posture. Take a few deep breaths and notice how you feel right now. Remember, it's okay to feel however you feel.

2. Let your breathing return to normal. Notice how your body feels.

3. Bring to mind someone you care about or love. This can be someone in your family, a friend, or even someone you've never met but admire. You can even choose a pet or a favorite animal. If you can't think of anyone, don't worry—it happens! Simply focus on the wish to be happy or the intention to send positive thoughts into the world.

4. Fully picture this person in your mind. Imagine laughing with them or doing something that makes them happy. Notice how you feel as you focus on this person.

5. Think about all of the good things you would wish for this person.

6. Use these phrases (or make up your own) to send this person kind wishes:

> *I wish for you to be happy.*
> *I wish for you to feel good.*
> *I wish for you to be peaceful.*

7. Imagine this person can really sense your good wishes. Notice how that feels.

8. You can focus on only this one person, or you can include others. You might choose to send kind thoughts to people close to you or others you might not normally consider (a teacher, the bus driver, the barista who makes your coffee).

9. Use the last part of this meditation to send kind thoughts to yourself.

> *I wish to be happy.*
> *I wish to be healthy.*
> *I wish to feel good.*

Try to soak in those good wishes.

10. Take a few deep breaths and another moment to notice how you feel right now.

CHANGE IT UP

Try this practice as something you do casually throughout your day. See if you can replace negative thoughts
like "there's something wrong with me" or "I'll never get a
girlfriend/boyfriend" with "I wish to be happy." Check out
what happens if you send kind thoughts to other drivers
instead of wanting to flip them off. It's actually really
powerful to consider that every single person you
see is just doing their best and could benefit from a
little kindness.

The "Don't Meditate" Practice

Meditation is a powerful tool to train your brain. Yet sometimes it isn't the right thing to do (at least at first). This "un-meditation" practice is for when you feel really triggered, or when your nervous system is either over- or under-activated. Over-activated feels like you're jumping out of your skin, totally wired, jittery, manic, losing it, or angry. You feel like punching something or running away. Under-activated is when you're totally numb or when everything feels like it's happening to someone else. For those times, you need to bring your system back "online" before you can do pretty much anything else. One of the best ways to do that is to move your body.

1. As gently as you can, notice how you feel. Maybe you tried to meditate, but it just feels totally impossible and overwhelming. Maybe you recently got some bad news, you're having trouble doing anything, or you just feel like nothing is going right and you want to run away.

2. The next step is to do something that gets you out of that space but isn't strenuous or burdensome. Find some way to be active that feels easy enough right now: throwing a ball around, dancing, going for a walk, or practicing gentle yoga.

CONTINUED

3. Don't worry about being mindful or meditating. Just let yourself do the activity.

4. When you feel ready, you might choose to do a Soaking in the Good (page 31), Body Scan (page 24), or kindness meditation, or find someone to talk to about what's going on.

BUDDY UP

You probably have a friend or family member who could use some help grounding or just making it through a difficult time. You might suggest helping each other when you need it. You don't even have to talk. Give each other the chance to be while you listen to music or shoot hoops.

The human brain seems rigged against teenagers. Your brain's alarm bell (amygdala) is fully developed when you're a baby, but the emotion-regulating part (prefrontal cortex) doesn't mature until about age 25 (see page 58). If you ever feel overly emotional or can't explain why you did something, it's actually your brain's wiring.

How can you work with this? Research shows you can make emotions less overwhelming simply by naming them. Acknowledging emotions reduces their power and lets you respond deliberately rather than feeling hijacked.

1. Find a comfortable posture. Even if your mind is restless or you feel overly emotional, try to find some gentleness in your body. If you can't sit still, you might choose to sway or walk slowly.

2. Take a few deep breaths, feeling what it's like to breathe.

3. Let your breathing be natural and notice how your body feels.

4. However you feel, try to notice it just as it is, without needing to eliminate it, figure it out, or change it in any way.

CONTINUED

5. When you're ready, gently ask yourself, "What am I feeling right now?" You don't have to come up with the perfect answer. It doesn't even have to be a word. Try to give a name (aloud or in your head) for how you feel right now.

6. Then explore how it feels in your body. What does anger feel like? Where do you feel sadness or joy? Is boredom heavy or light?

7. As you pay attention to the emotion, you might notice that it changes and that your mind doesn't want to stay with your body. Your mind might get caught up in thinking, blaming, or worrying. That's okay. You can name those emotions or actions, too. And whenever you notice your mind has wandered, gently bring your attention back to your breathing, your body, and this moment right now.

8. When you're finished, notice how you feel. You might even name that, too.

AM I DOING THIS RIGHT?

This practice may make you feel vulnerable because you're facing emotions that may be challenging. Know that the exercise isn't creating any emotions; it's just letting the ones that are present be felt. If it feels like too much, you can always come back to breathing awareness or connecting to the external environment with your senses.

This meditation helps you become familiar with your patterns. Whenever sadness, frustration, or big emotions arise, see if you can give them a name, noticing how they feel. You can even get creative with the names: Fed-up Fatima, Horrible Harry, etc.

Being with Things in a Different Way—R.A.I.N.

Sometimes it can feel like you're one big ball of emotions, thoughts, or even pain, and it's too much. This practice, created by Michele Donald, lets you see those experiences directly, being curious about them without judging them or overidentifying with them. They're just something that's happening, not a declaration of who you are.

1. As always, find a posture that feels comfortable and sustainable. Take a few deep breaths and notice what it feels like to breathe.

2. Let your breathing be natural.

3. Take a moment to explore what it's like to be you right now.

4. Let your attention settle by doing some mindful breathing or a body scan.

5. When you feel ready, you'll notice that there's a lot going on in your awareness. When something big arises and sticks around, turn your attention toward that and mindfully check it out.

6. Whatever you notice, use the R.A.I.N. technique to explore it:

R: Recognize. Notice what's there. What's happening right now?

A: Allow, accept. You don't need to fight it, change it, or figure it out. Just see if you can let it be there without trying to make anything happen.

I: Investigate with kindness. Check out what it feels like in your body. How does it move? What's its temperature or color? Where are its edges? Is it fast or slow? Heavy or light? Try to investigate kindly, not critically.

N: Not me, non-identification. Whatever it is, it isn't you. You don't have to judge yourself for having it around. It's only a visitor that's hanging out for a bit.

7. When that sensation or emotion dissipates, come back to your breath and body until you finish or choose to focus on another experience.

TAKE IT FURTHER

You'll likely have a few recurring emotional states or physical pains. Try to explore those common discomforts with this practice. See if you can be curious about them rather than disliking them or thinking there's something wrong with you for having them. It's pretty empowering to give yourself permission to cry or feel however you feel.

Self-Compassion

Mindfulness is actually pretty radical. It's asking you to befriend the parts of yourself and your life you might otherwise hate or beat yourself up about. It asks you to be gentle when being judgmental is easier.

Self-compassion is all about that gentle approach. It's about holding yourself the way you'd hold a small animal or child, or the way you want a loved one to hold you when you're down. Studies show it can increase overall well-being and reduce symptoms of depression and anxiety. It's not about getting rid of bad feelings, but rather choosing a kinder response. It has three parts: kindness, mindfulness, and common humanity.

1. Pause and take a breath or two. Notice how you feel in your body.

2. Let your breathing be natural.

3. Start by focusing on breathing or your senses.

4. Imagine you can inhale kindness and compassion, and exhale whatever is hard right now. Every exhalation is a chance to let go.

5. When you're ready, gently ask yourself, "What do I need to hear right now? What are the most supportive words someone could tell me?" You don't have to look for an answer. Just let whatever arises be there. Imagine that you're asking for someone you love who's in pain.

6. If no words come, or if you prefer, you can use a version of these phrases:

> *I'm okay. I don't have to solve this right now. It's okay to feel like this.* (Kindness)
> *This is a moment of suffering. This is really hard. This moment hurts.* (Mindfulness)
> *I'm not alone. There is nothing wrong with me. Other people feel this way, too.*
> (Common Humanity)

7. Repeat your own or any of these phrases as much as you need.

8. If you feel tension in your body or if big emotions come up, you might ask: "What is my body telling me right now?" or "What parts of me need kindness right now?" You can direct those kind words to whatever parts of you need it most. You might incorporate the Self-Soothing Practices (page 50) exercise.

CONTINUED

9. As you finish, imagine someone who loves you or someone you love giving you a big hug, stroking your hair, or telling you it's okay. Let yourself feel really supported. Try to care for yourself as gently as you would care for a friend in need.

10. Take a few more deep breaths.

TAKE IT FURTHER

The times when we most need to be a friend to ourselves are usually the times it's hardest to remember to do it. Take a moment when you're feeling okay to write yourself a letter or an e-mail with the things you most need or want to hear when you're struggling. Then keep it in a safe place that you'll come back to when you need it.

It's Okay Not to Be Okay

No one really likes feeling bad. But the thing is, emotions aren't actually bad or good. We just like some of them more than others. If you've ever felt good when you've cried or had a "pity party," then you know this. Emotions really need to be felt before you can do anything about them.

The famous psychoanalyst Carl Jung said, "What you resist not only persists, but will grow in size." Mindfulness teacher Shinzen Young describes it as an equation: Suffering = pain × resistance. Basically: The more you fight stuff you don't like, the bigger it gets and the more it makes you suffer. That doesn't mean you have to *like* feeling bad or indulge it. It's just seeing that fighting only makes you feel worse. Practicing this way, you don't have to feel bad for feeling bad.

1. Find a place where you feel safe and can be undisturbed for a few minutes.

2. Take a few deep breaths. If you feel really triggered or activated, you might choose to spend some time with the practices on page 132 before proceeding.

CONTINUED

3. Let your breathing be normal. Notice how your body feels right now. Notice any contact with the furniture or floor, and any areas of tension you can release.

4. However you feel, whatever's going on, remind yourself that it's okay. You can even tell yourself, "It's okay to feel this way. It's okay not to feel okay."

5. See if you can turn toward this feeling rather than ignoring or resisting it. You might imagine it's a good friend who's really struggling. You wouldn't just say, "Go away" or "What's wrong with you?" You would be gentle and reassuring.

6. This might bring up tears or different emotions or sensations. Those are totally normal. It's just your nervous system letting go of stress. Try to be gentle with those, too.

7. Take a few more deep breaths. Notice how you feel now.

TAKE IT FURTHER

When you're in the thick of something big or unpleasant, it feels like it will last forever. If you deal with depression or anxiety, you know that feeling of being convinced you'll never be all right again. As you explore this practice, look for not only the feelings themselves, but also how they move and change. This helps you see that even the hardest moments aren't static, regardless of what you might believe at the time. Turning toward these feelings with compassion, remind yourself that you won't always feel this way. You might say this or a phrase that really resonates with you out loud: "This is just a moment." "I can get through this even if I don't feel like it."

It definitely takes practice to be with discomfort rather than resisting it. Try this for little frustrating things (when your siblings are being annoying or you have to get up early), so that you have this skill when you really need it.

Self-Soothing Practices

For that feeling when you're really triggered, like there's too much going on, or you need to release some stress or anxiety—explore these self-soothing postures along with (or separate from) your meditation. Your nervous system is wired to be soothed by gentle touch. See how these fit for you.

1. Find a place where you feel safe. (If you feel really overwhelmed, it can be helpful to have someone you trust with you.) Lie down if that feels okay, otherwise take a posture that feels comfortable.

2. Take a few deep breaths if you can.

3. Let your breathing be natural.

4. Choose one of the postures described on page 51 and follow the instructions.

5. Notice how you feel in this position. Be mindful of your body and/or your breath going in and out.

6. If it ever feels like too much, take a break. Remind yourself that you're okay. Let things settle.

7. Stay in the posture as long as you like. Notice how you feel when you're done.

POSTURE ONE: SELF-HOLD/HUG (HELPFUL FOR TOO MUCH ENERGY/ADHD)

1. Basically, you're giving yourself a hug. Put your right hand across your body on your back below your armpit (near your heart). Put your left arm across your body on top, touching your opposite arm (on your triceps muscle).

2. Notice how you feel. Remind yourself that it's okay to feel however you feel. Really focus on caring for yourself. You're hugging yourself the way you would hug friends if they were really hurting.

3. Practice mindfulness of breathing or your body and senses in this posture.

POSTURE TWO: HANDS ON HEAD/HEART/BELLY (VERY SOOTHING OVERALL)

1. Put one hand on your forehead and one on your chest near your heart. Feel the touch of your hands on your body.

2. Feel what happens between your hands. Notice any flow of energy or change of temperature. You might imagine there is a river flowing in between them.

3. Next, take your hand off your forehead and put it on your belly or diaphragm. Notice how that touch feels.

CONTINUED

4. Again, notice any flow of energy between your hands. Check out any shifts or movement.

5. As before, see if you can really rest in this posture. Let yourself be soothed and feel cared for.

CHANGE IT UP

Here's a secret: No one can tell if you put one hand on your abdomen while you're sitting down, and it can make a huge difference in how you feel. It can be really helpful before a test, audition, difficult conversation, or play-off game. Experiment with the positions that feel most comforting to you.

Research conducted by psychologist Sonja Lyubomirsky suggests that while 50 percent of happiness is genetically predetermined and 10 percent is due to external circumstances, a full 40 percent is the result of your own personal outlook. That means 90 percent of happiness is not about having the most things, the most likes, or being the most conventionally beautiful. For the 40 percent you can control, it's all about how you relate to yourself and the world.

Practicing gratitude improves physical and mental health, eases depression, and increases well-being, including feelings of satisfaction with your life and your interpersonal relationships.

1. Start with a few deep breaths, bringing yourself back to the present moment.

2. Breathing naturally, notice how it feels to pause and be still.

3. Look for something you are grateful for, something you appreciate, something that makes you happy, or just something that's interesting. It can be big or small. You can use something you see or connect to in your environment, or something in your mind or memory.

CONTINUED

4. Check out how being grateful makes you feel in your body. Notice what it's like to think about a friend or just appreciate the sun on your face. Even if something smells bad, you can appreciate the ability of your nose and brain to perceive that smell. You can be grateful for one tiny moment of quiet before your brother starts playing on his iPad.

5. If you can't come up with anything (which happens), you can be grateful for the chance to pause for this moment and just be.

6. Take the final moment of the practice to be grateful for your ability to stop and notice.

TAKE IT FURTHER

This is a great habit to practice regularly, because the more you look for things to be grateful for, the better you generally feel. Try to keep a gratitude journal that you write in regularly, or partner up with a friend and text each other three gratitudes each day.

You Are Not Your Thoughts

> **"Don't believe everything you think. Thoughts are just that–thoughts."**
> **ALLAN LOKOS**

The goal of meditation isn't to control your thoughts; it's to stop letting them control you. You do this by paying attention to the process of thinking rather than the content of the thought, and by seeing that you are not your thoughts and they don't define you.

The idea is to watch thoughts the way you'd watch passing cars as you stand on the sidewalk. Let them come and go without hitching a ride. And when you find yourself thinking (i.e., taking a ride), you get to see it and choose to come back to the sidewalk (let go of the thought) at any time.

1. Notice what you feel as you take a few deep breaths.

2. Letting your breath be natural, use it as your anchor and feel what it's like to breathe.

3. As thoughts arise, try to let them come and go without getting caught up in their story. You can have thoughts without really thinking them.

CONTINUED

4. Whenever you notice you have been thinking, see how your body feels. As soon as you notice thinking, you're actually back in the present moment. You can't control your mind wandering, but you can choose your response when you see it.

5. If you feel like you're stuck in a thought or worry, and it won't just come and go, see if you can explore what it feels like instead of trying to get rid of it, diving into it, or beating yourself up for having it. What's really happening? What emotions are connected to it? How do those feel in your body?

6. As much as possible, explore what's happening in your body, rather than in your mind. What do you feel? What can you notice? Explore pace, temperature, heaviness, pressure, movement, and more. You might have a thousand thoughts in five minutes. That's totally normal. Every thought that comes up is a chance to be kind to yourself and to choose your focus.

7. It can be helpful here to name or label those thoughts that you get stuck in. It's another way to notice the thought without getting caught up in it.

8. When you finish, take a few more deep breaths and notice how you feel.

TAKE IT FURTHER

Start looking for and exploring the most common stories your mind tells you. Maybe *what if* is the first thing that arises whenever anything happens: "What if I fail?" "What if I can't do it?" Maybe you assume the worst or see everything in black and white: "This is never going to work." The goal isn't analysis but instead becoming familiar with your patterns, so whenever you start down that path you can notice that it's not the truth; it's just a habit. Then you can decide which thoughts you believe and which ones you can let go of.

Know Your Brain: Your Brain on Meditation

What does meditation actually do to your brain? Although this is a blooming field of complex research, we can cover some of the basic brain anatomy that is affected by meditation. There are a few key areas that are helpful to know:

Prefrontal cortex (PFC): It's the CEO of the brain, responsible for decision-making, regulating emotions, and modulating fear. When you want to lash out at someone in anger but stop because you realize it won't help, that's the PFC in action. It helps us make good decisions, plan for the future, and have impulse control, willpower, and self-awareness. It's not fully developed until your mid-20s.

With mindfulness, your PFC becomes thicker, which makes you better at regulating your emotions (keeping you more balanced and less freaked out) and helps you make better decisions. You get to respond the way you want rather than being at the mercy of your automatic reactions.

Amygdala: It's the sounder of the alarm. When it thinks you are threatened, it calls for the release of hormones to make sure you can fight or run. It wants to protect you at all costs, but it's really overactive and overeager. It protects you from things that aren't even a threat. When the amygdala is fired up, it's really hard to access the PFC, which is why you yell at someone when you're really emotional even though some part of you knows it's not a good idea.

With mindfulness meditation, your amygdala fires less often. It gets triggered less easily and is less activated. That means you are less stressed out.

Hippocampus: This part of your brain is involved with learning, awareness, and memory. If you've ever studied for a test and know the answer, but your brain can't bring it to the surface, you've seen how stress can hijack your hippocampus. The more stressed you are (e.g., the more your amygdala is firing), the less likely you are to access the information stored in your hippocampus.

Mindfulness meditators were found to have increased gray matter in the area of the hippocampus, meaning they have better working memory.

CHAPTER THREE

Meditations for School Life

> *"The basic root of happiness lies in our minds;*
> *outer circumstances are nothing more*
> *than adverse or favorable."*
> **MATTHIEU RICARD**
>
> *"How you look at it is pretty much how you'll see it."*
> **RASHEED OGUNLARU**

If you find school stressful, you aren't alone. Eighty-three percent of students surveyed by the American Psychological Association report that school is a significant or somewhat significant source of stress, affecting mental and physical health and grades.

Right now, school is probably a fact of your life. You can't do much about it. But you can do something about how you approach it. You might still have stress (grade expectations, homework, or difficult friends), but you'll be less stressed out (feeling like there's something wrong with you, like you'll never pass, or like everyone but you knows what they're doing). You can use mindfulness to notice what's happening and then to be nicer to yourself as you face the inevitable challenges in your school day. That means *you* get to be in charge—not the bully in your brain, not your friends, and not the overwhelming nervousness you get before a test or starting something new. Mindfulness helps you choose how you want school to affect your life.

Starting a New Class

New things can be scary. The key is not to fight the fear or worry. Instead, choose to see them, even say hi, and let them be there. You might not like them, but this way they don't push you over because you're aware that they're there and you don't need to resist them. Worry is your brain's attempt to solve an unsolvable problem. It compounds problems rather than fixing them. Worrying activates the brain's reward centers because it gives the brain something to do. Instead of getting caught in that feedback loop, notice it and come back to what's happening right now—your body, senses, and breath in this moment.

1. Start with a breath meditation, body scan, or sensory practice like Be Here Now (page 26) or Soaking in the Good (page 31). Notice your body, senses, and mind right now.

2. Notice any stories or judgments that are going through your mind about yourself, other people, or the class.

3. See if you can breathe with those thoughts. Let them come and go like clouds moving in the sky. You don't control them, and you don't have to believe them. Come back to the feeling in your body rather than getting caught up in the story of those thoughts.

4. If you feel nervous or scared, that's okay, too. Just notice what it feels like to have nervousness. You can even say that to yourself, "I'm not nervous. I just have some nervousness right now."

5. Turn your attention to the feeling of this moment rather than your assessment of it.

6. Try some self-compassion as you take a few more deep breaths.

TAKE IT FURTHER

Use this technique for any new class or experience. Whenever you notice your mind getting ahead of you, try to slow down deliberately and take things one step at a time. Just this breath. Just this moment. Just this introduction. Then, just that first class. Just the next moment and the next. At each turn, you might be tempted to make conclusions about how this is going, how you're doing, or what will happen in the future. When those come up, see if you can feel your body breathing and your feet on the floor. Notice, *this is what is happening right now*, and the thoughts aren't the truth of this moment.

Taking an Exam

You've studied for the test. You know your stuff. But when you get to the exam and pick up your pen, what happens? Your mind goes blank. And the harder you try, the more you feel stressed and the more inaccessible the answers seem to be. Sound familiar? When you're stressed, it's much harder to access the parts of your brain where memories (including test answers) are stored. Whether you get nervous before, during, or after a test, you can use this practice to help bring your mind back online.

1. Start with a quick breath, body scan, or Be Here Now meditation (page 26).

2. Picture the classroom where the test happens. Imagine sitting there with the paper in front of you. Notice how your body feels.

3. Take a few deeper breaths. Imagine you could breathe out some of your tension or stress.

4. Picture yourself taking the test with ease and focus. What would it be like to feel confident that you knew the answers?

5. Imagine you can breathe in calm and focus, and breathe out any nerves or worries.

6. Continue to breathe and focus this way for as long as you like. Remember that you have these tools whenever you need them. If the nervousness starts to feel overwhelming, name it (page 39), remind yourself that you're okay, and then bring your attention to a neutral part of your body and take a few deeper breaths.

CHANGE IT UP

You can do this meditation as preparation before a test (or any big event). You can also do it right before you begin or even during the test itself. Remember that your breath and body are your anchors, so when your mind starts to run away with you, you can always come back to breathing or the feeling of your feet. It's okay to feel nervous, upset, or scared. This exercise helps you avoid being nervous, upset, or scared about being nervous, upset, or scared.

Coping with Mistakes

Here are two facts of life: 1) You are human. 2) Humans make mistakes. The thing is that the mistake isn't a fixed commentary on who you are. It's just something that happened. With mindfulness, the mistake can be less of a reaction ("I'm an idiot") and more of a mindful response ("I made a mistake. And it sucks. But it happened"). Until someone invents a time machine, you can't change the past. And beating yourself up doesn't do anything except make you feel worse. But you can still do something. You can learn a lesson, fix whatever's necessary (apologize, make amends), forgive yourself, and move on.

1. Take a few deep breaths.

2. Slow down. Try a self-compassion meditation or a self-soothing posture.

3. Remind yourself of (or practice) the It's Okay Not to Be Okay practice (page 47).

4. Notice how any discomfort, frustration, or shame feels in your body. Try to let those feelings be present without beating yourself up for having them.

5. Remind yourself that you can't change what happened, but you can choose how you respond.

6. Ask yourself if there's a lesson to learn here. Instead of ruminating on the past, see what you can do to change the future. Do you need to do something to make amends? Can you apologize (to yourself or someone else)? How can you forgive yourself and move on? Maybe you actually need to feel that discomfort, name it, and see that you are more than it, even if it feels awful. Maybe you need to tell yourself something like: "I made a mistake. It feels terrible. I'm going to do x, y, z next time. Beating myself up about this won't change anything."

7. Whenever you start to replay the mistake over again, choose some self-compassion or spend some time on a body scan. Come back to these anchoring compassion practices whenever you need them.

TAKE IT FURTHER

Pair this practice with the Finding Forgiveness practice on page 82 to give yourself the freedom to make mistakes, learn from them, and move forward. As with other people, it's incredibly powerful to see that just because you did something bad doesn't mean you're a bad person. What does it take to forgive yourself and see yourself as more than just some mistakes?

Preparing for a Big Game or Performance

Like a new class, this exercise is about seeing what's alive in any moment and letting it be. Athletes use meditation as a way to find their own calm amid the madness of fans, lights, and noise. Do an Internet search for "LeBron James meditating" to see one of the best basketball players totally centered when everything around him is in chaos. Use this meditation as a way to find your own eye of the storm. Whatever is happening around you and in you is okay, and you can acknowledge it without it throwing you off balance.

1. Start with a body or breath meditation.

2. Noticing how you feel, see if you can apply the R.A.I.N. practice (page 42) to whatever is going on.

3. Check out all of the things that are going on inside you and around you, and remind yourself you are deciding what to focus on.

4. Turn to what feels most solid and stable in your awareness. That might be your breath, the feeling of your feet on the ground, or the sounds you hear. You can even remind yourself, "This feeling is okay, and I can hang out here in the eye of this storm."

5. Then really use the feeling of breathing and of your body to anchor your attention. Put all of your awareness on these stable anchors. Let your breath be like the waves in the ocean. The world might be intense, but the breath always goes in and out. The expectations might be overwhelming, but your feet are solid on the ground.

TAKE IT FURTHER

You can use this practice as a visualization before a big game or performance. Use your mind and senses to fully picture yourself at the game or show. Notice how your body feels as you warm up or prep. Imagine all the noise and chaos that might be going on and choose to bring your focus back to your own body and senses. Whenever you get distracted, notice it and kindly come back to your chosen focus.

Finding Balance

Much of life is about finding the balance between two much effort and not enough. It's like playing guitar: If your strings are too loose, there's no sound; too tight and they'll break. Meditation and schoolwork require that same balance. For meditation, if your body is too tight, you'll get stressed; too loose or relaxed, you'll fall asleep. If you expect results, you'll get tense and likely disappointed. If you don't try at all, you'll never get the experience of seeing yourself and the world in a new way. For school, if you are too lax, you won't get stuff done; too tense and you'll crack under pressure. Balance is the key here.

Take a moment to pause, whether you're in the middle of work, meditation, or another activity. Notice your body and breath. Check out what your mind is telling you.

IF YOU'RE WORKING AND STARTING TO FEEL STRESSED:

1. Notice your breathing. Do a quick breath meditation and anchor your attention to the feeling of breathing.

2. Notice the speed or pace of your mind. If you feel like you can't stop or it feels frenetic, that's a good indication that you need a moment to pause.

3. Ask yourself, "What do I need right now?"

4. If you do pause, give yourself full permission to take a break. "I'm giving myself five minutes to reenergize, so I can come back less stressed and more balanced."

5. Take that time to be still and focus on your breathing or senses, or go for a walk and notice what's around you. (Hint: Looking at your phone doesn't actually give your brain a break, even if it feels like it does.)

6. Then come back to work refreshed. Make the commitment to keep going.

IF YOU'RE IN THE MIDDLE OF SOMETHING, AND YOU FEEL DISENGAGED OR SPACED OUT:

1. Again, pause and notice what's happening in your body and mind.

2. Take a few deep breaths and let yourself feel the breath going in and out.

3. Feel your body in your chair and your feet on the floor.

4. Orient yourself to what's around you. What can you see, hear, smell, taste, and feel?

5. Then take a moment to renew your intention. Remind yourself what you are doing (training your mind, learning new skills, working toward graduation).

6. As you come back to the task, remind yourself, "I got this."

TAKE IT FURTHER

One of the best skills you can learn is to trust when you need to take a break and when you need to push yourself. Try experimenting with that balance throughout your day. As you start to get frustrated with traffic, see if you can pause. As you find yourself binge-watching a show, see if you can check in with what you really need in that moment.

Navigating Uncertainty

Your brain is pretty terrible at predicting the future. It gets convinced you're going to fail a test before you take it. It can believe someone hates you before you've even spoken to them. When it doesn't know what's going on, it usually predicts the worst. The main idea here is that it's okay not to know what's next. It's okay to have no idea what you want to be when you grow up. Almost every adult you meet is doing a totally different job than they thought they were going to do! So you get to change your relationship to uncertainty, seeing that it shows up as discomfort in your body and incessant commentary in your mind. While those things might not be pleasant, they can simply be sensations to notice before deciding how you want to respond to them.

1. Start by taking a second to orient yourself to this moment by paying attention to your senses as they are right now.

2. You might incorporate one of the practices from chapter 2 that feels right for the moment. Maybe you need some compassion or anchoring to your breath or just a simple check-in with your body.

CONTINUED

3. When you're ready, see if you can notice what it feels like not to know or to be uncertain. Notice where you feel that uncertainty in your body. See if you can be kind and curious when you notice what's there.

4. You can use a version of the Naming Emotions practice (page 39). You might say: "Uncertainty feels like this." "Right now, uncertainty is sitting in my stomach, and it feels heavy."

5. Remind yourself that it's okay and that you aren't alone in your uncertainty. Everyone is lost about one thing or another. It's not just you.

6. See if you can bring in some gratitude or compassion for where you are right now. You might think back to the last time you felt lost or uncertain, considering what you felt then and how you got through it.

7. As you finish, remind yourself that this discomfort is only another feeling. It's not the truth.

AM I DOING THIS RIGHT?

Uncertainty feels especially uncomfortable when it butts heads with your expectations. It feels so bad because there's an expectation that you should know or that this moment shouldn't be like this. Try to notice those "shoulds" as thoughts that can come and go if you let them.

Seeing Procrastination for What It Is

Procrastination is all about avoiding or delaying discomfort. You go on Instagram because your mind says it's better (easier) than doing work. Meditation lets you see that this discomfort isn't so bad. The worst part isn't the experience itself but your mind's resistance—the fact that your mind has already decided that it's going to be terrible. It's worse in your head than in reality.

Mindfulness is the antidote here, because it lets you see your patterns and decide which ones are helpful or not. It lets you see that the discomfort and anxiety are just thoughts and feelings, and you can decide how to respond to those. Then you can get on with your work, because you aren't resisting what's really happening.

1. Start with a few deep breaths.

2. Let your breathing be natural.

3. Take a few moments to breathe and notice what that feels like. Let go of the distraction and the task and just be with the feeling of your body breathing.

4. Notice what's going on in your mind. What stories is your mind telling you? Check out what it feels like in your body to be avoiding the work that's ahead of you.

CONTINUED

5. Turning toward the feelings, see if you can really be with what's going on in your body. Use R.A.I.N. (page 42) to explore whatever's alive and allow it to be there.

6. Whenever your mind wanders or you start judging, complete this phrase: "Right now, I'm aware of x or y and it's okay." ("Right now, I'm aware of being hungry. Right now, I'm aware of feeling guilty. Right now, I'm aware of birds chirping.")

7. Whatever you are aware of, notice it with kindness and compassion. Notice that however uncomfortable those feelings of doing or not doing work are, you are still stronger than them.

8. As you finish, take a moment to set an intention for what you'll do with your time now.

CHANGE IT UP

Even with the best intentions, most of us still procrastinate. It's fine to take breaks or to give yourself time to chill out. To build better habits, set time limits (and commit to sticking to them). Set the timer on your phone for 30 minutes, during which time you can do whatever you want that isn't work. When the timer goes off, you've made the commitment to getting the job done. If it's helpful, you can set blocks of time—first to chill, then to work, then to take a break, then more work.

Staying Present for Class or Homework

Research shows that the more our minds stay on the task at hand, the happier we actually are, regardless of what the task itself is! You can't get rid of homework, chores, or the parts of your job you dislike or find tedious, but you can change how you approach them.

The way to deal with boredom is to first see it as just another judgment of your mind and then find anything you can be curious about in this moment.

1. Start with a breath or body meditation.

2. Choose to use this time to notice and be with what's happening without trying to change it, get rid of it, or judge it.

3. Notice how you feel right now.

4. Use your senses to explore this moment. Washing dishes, doing homework, or performing any other task can become interesting if you decide to find something interesting about it.

5. Ask yourself, "What can I be interested in right now? What are my senses telling me?"

CONTINUED

6. Whenever your mind goes back into *this is boring* mode, see if you can notice that as only a thought and come back to the physical experience of the task at hand or even just your breath or body position.

TAKE IT FURTHER

This practice gets at the heart of mindful exploration, because it's all about changing your automatic response to a stimulus. And it lets you see that you are in control of your mind and your relationship to the world. Take it deeper by exploring as many of your automatic judgments as you like. Start to notice (and not judge) what immediate thoughts come up when you look at someone new, hear a sound, or listen to your teachers. Consider: What could you learn from this person or this moment?

Know Your Brain: Negativity Bias

If you've ever focused on the negative more than the positive or felt like only one bad thing got stuck in your brain and ruined your otherwise good day, you've already experienced the negativity bias.

It's that habit we all have where we see, focus on, and remember the negative more than the positive. It's actually hardwired into our brains. Our ancestors needed this adaptation in order to survive in a very dangerous environment. Their brains (and ours) developed an uncanny ability to look for and respond to threats (which would activate their fight-or-flight mode, see page 99). If they mistook a rope for a snake, they'd be on edge, but safe. But if they thought the dangerous snake was just a harmless rope, it was game over. So your brain actually looks for the negative as a way to protect you.

What that means is you don't have to blame yourself or feel like there's something wrong with you if you see the bad more than the good. It's not just you! And you can train your brain to counteract the negativity bias by being mindful, practicing gratitude, and seeking out the good in your life and the world. The more you focus on and look for the good, the more you train your brain to see it.

CHAPTER FOUR

Meditations
for Friends
and Family

> *"Be kind whenever possible. It is always possible."*
> **DALAI LAMA**

Family and friends can be so challenging because you can love them and hate them, almost at the same time. To be in a relationship of any kind requires being open to your own as well as the other person's perspective, faults, and needs. It takes patience, kindness, acceptance, and interest—all of the things you are training when you do these mindfulness practices. Meditations for friends and family focus on building kindness and seeing that we are all human beings doing our best.

Finding Forgiveness

> *"Forgiveness means giving up all hope for a better past."*
> **JACK KORNFIELD**

Forgive and forget. That's the saying, right? Yet this practice isn't asking you to forget. And it isn't asking you to pretend something didn't happen or to condone it. The idea is to forgive because you recognize that the only person who really suffers when you hold on to anger is you. It's like that old saying: "Being angry at someone else is like holding fire in your hand and expecting it to burn the other person." This practice lets you be free from all of that.

1. Find a comfortable, upright posture and take a few deep breaths.

2. Noticing how you feel right now, let your breathing be natural.

3. Take a few moments to bring yourself into the present moment by attending to your breath and body.

4. When you're ready, bring to mind the situation at hand.

5. Gently turning toward any pain or discomfort, notice any and all experiences that arise. Name any emotions, check out any automatic judgments, and notice any sensations in your body.

6. Notice if you get stuck replaying the story of what happened or if you're arguing your case: "It shouldn't have happened, they were wrong, I can't believe they did that to me." Then return to the emotions and sensations that are present right now.

7. As you acknowledge the discomfort, make a commitment to freely offer your forgiveness to this person (or yourself). In your mind you might say:

> *I forgive you for making a mistake.*
> *I forgive you for causing me pain.*
> *I forgive you for not seeing how much it hurt.*

8. If you are the one who wronged someone else, turn toward your own need for caring and compassion. In your mind, say, "I forgive myself for hurting them. I forgive myself for making a mistake."

9. Practices like this can bring up all sorts of emotions. If you feel overwhelmed, come back to your breathing as your anchor or turn to some self-compassion. If it feels false or weird, remind yourself how it might help and see if you can do it anyway.

CONTINUED

10. When you're done, notice how you feel. Continue to make the commitment to show compassion for yourself and others and to find freedom amid the hurt.

AM I DOING THIS RIGHT?

Forgiveness doesn't mean that you let people take advantage of you or that you put up with anything. And forgiving yourself isn't letting yourself get away with anything. It's about how you're relating to something that's already happened and being free from something you can't change.

If someone is continually putting you down or hurting you in any way, you get to do what's best for you, including breaking ties with that person or getting other help. You might consider the Finding Forgiveness (page 82) or Seeing Past Differences practice (page 106) as ways to see the person mindfully—but that's to heal yourself, not to let them get away with causing you pain.

Have you ever had a conversation with someone where you could tell they weren't listening, but waiting to talk? Listening mindfully follows the same basic premise as all the other exercises. It's about being present in a kind, curious, nonjudgmental way and being open to what's happening rather than coming at it with preconceived ideas. Here, instead of doing all of that with your own body or emotions, you do it while listening to someone else. The goal is listening to understand, rather than listening to reply.

As you prepare for a conversation, or even in the middle of one if you get heated or distracted, take a moment to connect to the intention to really listen openly and receive what the other person is offering.

1. Pause at the start of the conversation and whenever you need to reconnect.

2. Try to worry less about exactly what you're going to say and really focus on listening first and foremost.

3. Whenever you notice yourself getting caught up in judgment or planning your next words, take a deep breath or two. Try to see those judgments as automatic thoughts that you can choose to believe or not.

CONTINUED

4. As you listen, see if you can notice when you're responding (being open to this other person's ideas whether you agree or not) and when you're reacting (being judgmental, getting caught up in taking something personally). Both are important to notice so you can decide what comes next.

5. During the discussion, check in with your perspective and make the effort to recognize that your point of view is different from anyone else's. Try to be open to seeing the world from the other person's perspective and to offering that person yours.

6. Every once in a while, you might ask yourself, "Can I openly listen to this person? Do I need to be right? Can I accept that this person doesn't agree with me?"

7. No matter how the conversation goes, when you can, take a moment to give yourself some gratitude for attempting this practice in the first place.

CHANGE IT UP

Listening—or hearing—is one of the greatest mindfulness tools, because it's always there and it's totally effortless. So, in addition to listening to other people, you might practice just listening to anything you can hear in any given moment. Let sound be merely sound without needing to identify it or decide what you think of it.

Having Challenging Conversations

Preparing for tough conversations begins with the same premise as forgiveness. You can't change the past, but you can change how it affects you in the present. Otherwise the past becomes like a prison that shuts you off and prevents you from healing. Forgiving, apologizing, and compassion release you from that prison.

Combine this with the Listening Mindfully practice (page 85) for a fully mindful conversation.

1. Start with a few deep breaths.

2. Let your breath be natural.

3. Take a moment to pause and feel your breath in your body and/or your feet on the ground. Deliberately relax your shoulders and release any tension in your jaw.

4. As you speak, take your time. It's okay to stop and take a breath. Relax and trust that what you need to say will come.

5. As with the Listening Mindfully practice, try to receive the other person's views openly, even if you disagree. Notice if you take things personally or expect the conversation to go a certain way, and then bring your attention back to hearing and breathing. Try to put yourself in that person's shoes.

CONTINUED

6. It's helpful to frame conversations so they're less about accusation and judgment and more about explanation and observation. Rather than saying, "You never let me see my friends," you might say, "When you tell me I can't go out, it makes me feel like you don't trust me." Then pause and let yourself really hear what the other person has to say.

7. If you're the one apologizing, try to see it as a gift you are offering freely—no strings attached. You can't control what the other person will do with your apology. Peace comes from offering the words without expectation.

8. If you feel resistance or the need to defend your position, try to acknowledge those without needing to believe them. Come back to your decision to find peace in the present moment.

9. Try to make clear requests about what you need now and in the future. What can this person help you with concretely? Ask them what they need and how you can facilitate that.

AM I DOING THIS RIGHT?

It's okay if this feels hard or a huge part of you doesn't want to do it. You get to allow that to be there and make the healthier choice anyway. Much of it is the conscious choice to set your ego aside (even if it doesn't want to go). You get to ask yourself, "Do I want to be right, or do I want to be happy?" That doesn't mean you always capitulate or give in. It means that you acknowledge that you're being imprisoned by the past, and you'll feel better by seeing that you have a choice for the present and the future.

Making Good Decisions

It makes sense that you want to fit in. From an evolutionary perspective, belonging meant safety, because anyone outside the group would have to fend for themselves. And yet, today it can feel like the pack (in person or online) is pushing you around more than supporting you.

Studies show that mindful meditation and deep breathing can actually help you make better decisions. Use this practice for decisions about peers or anything that's on your mind.

(If you're really depressed or anxious, it can feel impossible to see clearly enough to make any decisions. It's not your fault. Try to give yourself an extra few days or seek out help from someone you trust to find that clarity.)

1. Start by taking a few deep breaths, feeling your body as it is right now.

2. Let your breathing be natural and notice how you feel.

3. Give yourself time to do a breath or body meditation.

4. When you're ready, turn your attention to the decision at hand. Instead of trying to solve it, state it simply: "Do I want to switch schools?" "Should I join that group?" "Is this party/substance/message worth my time?"

5. As you make this inquiry, notice what happens. Check out any immediate feelings in your body.

6. As openly and kindly as possible, ask yourself, "How do I really feel about this? Is this good for me? Will this make me happy, or am I doing it because I think I should?" You don't need to search for answers, just let whatever arises be there.

7. Be open to whatever feelings or counterarguments come up. You might know that you want to stay home, but you feel like your friends want you to go out. Much of making decisions connected to peers is about being clear in your own mind about what's important to you and trusting your own judgment. At the same time, everyone has responsibilities, and some of that means doing stuff you don't want to do. Consider how you can make this decision so you stay true to yourself and do the right thing. Trust that you know yourself and you have wisdom here.

8. If you notice that your mind is churning the same thoughts over and over again, it's time to step back and come back to your body or orient to your external environment. Take a break, maybe go for a walk, and then come back to this when you feel ready.

CHANGE IT UP

If you're particularly stuck on a decision, you might ask yourself, how will I feel about this in five minutes? Five hours? Five days? This can offer some much-needed perspective, particularly because everything feels totally permanent when you're in the thick of it.

Handling Parental Expectations

Here's the truth: No one, including your parents, has it all figured out. They're likely feeling confused about your adolescence and perhaps are sad that you don't want to talk or spend as much time with them. And they might not have much of a clue how to handle it. Whatever your parents are expecting or doing, it's almost guaranteed they aren't doing it to hurt you deliberately.

It's likely that your parents have some unrealistic expectations about you; you probably have some about them. And, just like you, your parents get scared, disappointed, and frustrated when those expectations aren't met. Mindfulness can help you see these expectations, so you can decide how you want to be with your parents.

1. Start with a few deep breaths. Notice how your body feels.

2. Let your breath be natural. Feel your feet on the floor.

3. Remind yourself that your parents, like you, are human and make mistakes. Remember that your life goes easier when you aren't in conflict with them.

CONTINUED

4. If they're disappointed or you feel you can't meet their expectations, really take the time to notice how that feels in your body. Try to be with the sensations without fueling the story. Let yourself feel that discomfort or pain. There's nothing wrong with you for feeling this way.

5. Know that it could be an automatic reaction on their part. They get scared, just like you, and react. That doesn't excuse behaviors that hurt, but it does let you see that they are more than this one action.

6. Try some self-compassion or the "Seeing Past Differences" practice (page 106) in the next chapter to do your best to see everyone in the kindest light.

7. When you feel ready, do your best to communicate with them. Tell them how you feel, as openly and nonjudgmentally as possible (to help with this use the Listening Mindfully practice, page 85, and Having Challenging Conversations practice, page 87). However it goes, whatever you say, try to be with the moment kindly and compassionately.

TAKE IT FURTHER

Approach a discussion with your parents as an act of love, rather than defense. It's not easy, but you get to take control of your part of this with honest expressions of what you feel. Parents can't listen unless you tell them what's going on.

Admittedly, there's only so much you can do. They might have their minds made up about who and how you're supposed to be. Even so, you've done your part by sharing your views openly and giving them a chance to know what's going on with you. If they continue to be disappointed, first try to consider that they care about you and want the best for you. Then come back to self-compassion and feeling what's happening in your body. You can't change who they are; you can only change your own response.

Looking for the Good in Relationships

You've probably heard people say that relationships need work. One of the reasons for this is that we are hardwired to pay more attention to the things that go wrong (see page 79). A famous marriage counselor, John Gottman, discovered that couples who are happy in their relationships have five positive interactions for every negative one. This is helpful for all relationships, not just for married people.

Use this practice whenever you feel stuck in negative thinking about a friend or family member, or even for any unhelpful habit you'd like to change.

1. Take a few deep breaths and notice how you feel.

2. Let your breathing be normal.

3. While you might be really mad at someone, remind yourself that you feel better when you're on good terms. It's not about forgetting that they've hurt you, but rather choosing how you want to move forward.

4. While your brain will likely want to dwell on what's wrong, do your best to seek out counterexamples. You can look through pictures or old texts or remember times when you had fun or appreciated this person.

5. Even if it feels awkward or it feels like it's easier to stay mad, try to keep looking for those positives. When you find something, check out how it feels in your body. Notice if you are resisting changing your mind and explore what that feels like.

6. When you've found several examples, take a few more deep breaths and notice how you feel now. Maybe there's something you need to say to this person or something you want to write in a journal.

7. The last step is to take a moment to thank yourself for doing this activity. Whatever you think about it, what you've done is pretty remarkable. Instead of taking the easier route of staying with the predominant emotion, you've proactively decided how you want to be.

AM I DOING THIS RIGHT?

All relationships have ups and downs. This practice is about finding the good in the relationships that support you and your well-being. This is not about forgiving unforgivable actions or staying in a relationship that is hurting you. Trust your gut. If it's a little thing or a challenge you can work through, go for it. If you are being hurt, abused, belittled, or manipulated, look for the good in yourself, trust your instincts, and talk to someone you can depend on.

Research shows that gratitude enhances interpersonal relationships. For those relationships that are healthy and supportive, consider regularly writing gratitude letters or notes to people in your life.

Know Your Brain: The Stress Response

While it has a bad reputation, stress is actually good. It's your body's natural response to danger. When your brain senses a threat, your autonomic (automatic) nervous system jumps into action, causing your heart to beat faster, your pupils to dilate, and your body to release hormones like adrenaline. It's called the sympathetic nervous response, and it allows you to run like mad or fight for your life (fight-or-flight mode). When the threat is over, your parasympathetic nervous response is supposed to take over, letting things calm down and come back to normal.

The problem for a lot of us is that our brains over-activate (we got too skilled at the negativity bias), and we tend to see everything as a threat: not just wild animals chasing us, but also missing the bus, not getting enough likes on social media, or someone not saying hi in the halls. Mindfulness can help you deactivate your overtaxed nervous system. You might still have the stressors, but they won't have the same impact. That means your brain won't overreact, and you can respond in the way you want.

CHAPTER FIVE

Meditations for Everyday Life

> *"We are what we repeatedly do.*
> *Excellence, then, is not an act, but a habit."*
> **WILL DURANT**

Your brain is always rehearsing something. The more you say, "I hate my body" or "I'm dumb," the better your brain gets at believing that. The more you get angry in traffic or judge other people who look or sound different, the stronger that neural pathway gets. Your mind is like your social media feed. You get to decide what to block and what to follow. Whatever you follow will affect you (consciously or unconsciously) and influence how you see yourself and the world. Mindfulness lets you see and decide which habits you want to build and which you want to eliminate.

Finding Your Passion

One of the greatest joys in life is finding your own passion. It also happens to be a huge stressor, because you don't always know what you want to do, and you get a million messages about what you should or shouldn't do. Meditation can help you find some clarity about what you really love. It can also help with creativity, because you can let go of fixed ways of thinking and explore the world as it appears in that moment.

1. Find a comfortable posture and take a few deep breaths. Notice how it feels to breathe and be in your body.

2. Let your breathing be natural and focus on how you feel. Use your breath or sound as your anchor and rest your attention there.

3. When you're ready, let go of the anchor and allow your attention to be with whatever is predominant in your awareness.

4. If whatever you're noticing lasts for only a moment or two, just notice it and then let it go. But if it sticks around, try to pay attention to it as you would your breath, sound, or body sensations. See if you can be interested and curious about this experience just as it is. Notice it with all of your senses. What can you see, hear, smell, taste, and touch? What happens as you explore this stimulus?

5. When that sensation or stimulus disappears, come back to your anchor until another prominent experience arises for you to explore.

6. Once you've practiced this for a bit, you might gently ask yourself, "What do I really love to do? How does x or y make me feel? Is this something I want to work at no matter what anyone else says?" You don't have to try to answer these questions—let them be there and notice what happens as you bring them to mind. You can let them percolate for hours, days, or even weeks. See what arises when you don't need to force an answer.

7. As you finish, take a few more deep breaths and notice how you feel now.

AM I DOING THIS RIGHT?

Both finding your passion and meditation require a degree of letting go and trusting yourself. You don't have to know everything or have all the answers. It doesn't have to make sense. And it won't always feel all that nice. The idea is that you'll want to work at it because it makes a difference overall.

The Everyday Stuff Practice

You almost certainly have stuff in your life you'd rather not deal with. Doing chores, helping out with siblings, or working late—necessary tasks you'd prefer not to do. The key is to just do the activity, notice what your body feels like as you do it, and see if you can find something to be curious about, without adding resistance or commentary to it.

1. Wherever you are, take a moment to pause and recognize; then recognize and let go of any stories, judgments, or critiques.

2. Take a few deep breaths and let your body settle as much as possible.

3. Letting your breath be natural, place your attention in your body, particularly in your feet. Notice what it feels like to stand, even bending your knees a bit to feel more grounded.

4. As you engage in this everyday task at hand, try to keep your attention in your body, finding something to hold your interest. It might be how the steering wheel feels beneath your fingers or how the lawn mower vibrates in your hands while you cut the grass.

5. Your mind will likely keep wanting to make a story out of this task ("Why do I have to do this? No one else is working this hard."). Try to let those thoughts come and go, then come back to the feeling of your body in this place.

6. If you start to get annoyed or frustrated with the people around you, you might try sending them some kind thoughts (page 34). Send yourself some, too, if you feel particularly stuck in negative thinking.

7. As you finish, take a few deep breaths and notice what it feels like to be free of your usual frustrations with this activity.

TAKE IT FURTHER

If you start doing this practice regularly, you'll notice the same stories or judgments come up a lot. So when you're standing in line somewhere, instead of getting caught up in the whole "Why is this taking so long? I always pick the wrong line" story, you can just notice that thought as a thought, and then come back to this present moment where all you are really doing is standing, feeling your feet on the ground, and breathing. This frees you from the unhelpful habits you didn't even know you were building.

Seeing Past Differences

No one sees the world the same way you do. Everyone gets their unique perspectives from their own beliefs, backgrounds, experiences, values, parents, education, and more, which is pretty incredible when you think about it. Your perspective is completely unique to you. And while most people do their best to be nonjudgmental about others, it can be hard to identify with people who have different backgrounds, look unfamiliar, or have different values.

This practice helps you recognize your own perspective. It helps you see some of the judgments you might not even know you're making about other people and lets you focus on the things that you have in common with people who seem different, rather than the things that divide you.

1. Find a posture that feels comfortable and take a few deep breaths, feeling the breath go in and out of your body.

2. Let the breath be natural.

3. Check out how your body and mind feel right now.

4. When you're ready, bring someone to mind who feels different from you. That might be based on how they look, act, or sound; a group they belong to at school; or simply what you think of them.

5. Try to let go of your thoughts about this person or interactions you've had. Instead, simply picture this person and consider what you both have in common as people. What makes you both human? Just like you, this person gets scared and lost, feels wonderful, doubts themself, wants to be happy, etc.

6. Say to yourself:

> *This person has feelings, thoughts, a body, and a mind . . . just like me.*
> *This person is doing their best . . . just like me.*
> *This person makes mistakes . . . just like me.*
> *This person wants to be happy . . . just like me.*

You can make up your own words or phrases that feel right for you. Focus on what you share with this person. What makes you both vulnerable human beings trying your best?

7. Notice if this person feels more real after making these connections. Perhaps instead of being "a bad guy," you now see someone who is a fallible human, just like you.

8. Explore how this feels in your mind and body as you take a few more deep breaths.

TAKE IT FURTHER

You can pair this practice with the next one to help you deal with difficult or challenging people in your life—for instance, that kid in your class or person at work who drives you wild. Or when your siblings or parents just don't get it. It helps you recognize some of your automatic judgments or reactions about others, so you can have more say in how you relate to people who are both similar to and different from you.

Dealing with Difficult People

Whether it's at school, at work, on the bus, or in your own household, there will always be difficult people: people who don't like how you look, how you talk, or what you're doing—regardless of anything you do or who you are. Maybe this is because they're unhappy. Maybe it's because it's a full moon. The truth is, it's about them, not about you. As RuPaul says, "What other people think of me is none of my business."

We want to protect ourselves from difficult people, yet it helps to see that they're also struggling, just like us. This creates compassion and connection. Henry Wadsworth Longfellow said, "If we could read the secret history of our enemies, we should find in each man's life sorrow and suffering enough to disarm all hostility."

1. Pause. Breathe. Notice how it feels to be in your body.

2. Explore all of your senses in this moment without needing to change or solve anything.

3. When you're ready, bring someone to mind who is a difficult person in your life right now, noticing what happens in your mind and body. Try to be gentle and compassionate with whatever occurs.

CONTINUED

4. Pairing this practice with the previous one, Seeing Past Differences, notice what it's like to see this person as just another human being. Just like you, they feel lost, want love, and get confused.

5. Take a moment to recognize that, no matter what they are doing, it isn't about you. Even say aloud, "What they think of me is none of my business." That doesn't excuse pain they cause you, but it lets you get perspective. Their (wrong or hurtful) view of you doesn't diminish who you are.

6. Remind yourself that you can't control their actions, only your own response. You can notice what hurt feels like and then decide what you let affect you. (Feeling the hurt gently isn't the same as reacting to it or feeding it with angry thoughts.)

7. As you do this, come back to your body sensations and breath. Let those be your focus.

8. As you finish, take a few more breaths and notice how you feel.

9. When you're done, take a moment to either write down or consider aloud these questions: What do I need to do to care for myself? How does being with this person truly make me feel? Am I letting them dictate my emotions by reacting? What could I do when they start to really get to me?

BUDDY UP

At times, the healthiest thing is to protect yourself. A friend or family member can help with this. Talk to someone you trust in order to come up with a plan. Maybe you need to set boundaries or avoid the troublesome person. Maybe you choose to pause and feel your feet when a person you can't avoid gets to you. Sharing this with someone else helps you be compassionate with yourself and know you aren't alone.

Receiving Feedback

Getting feedback is a necessary part of your life. You get grades and test results at school, and evaluations at work, not to mention likes on social media. Yet it's likely no one has ever told you how to actually do this well. You're just supposed to be okay with whatever people tell you. Often, that's not easy at all.

The idea here is to take what's useful, discard what's not, and respond rather than react. A compliment becomes a gift. You can receive it and enjoy it without needing to keep getting more or basing who you are on what other people think of you. And a critique is an opportunity to use what's helpful and then reject any part that makes it a personal comment on who you are.

1. Take a few deep breaths. If you've received a compliment or critique, this helps you pause, break with your automatic reaction, and choose a different response.

2. Let your breathing be natural. Feel your feet on the ground and the temperature of your skin.

3. If you've received a compliment, notice how it feels in your body. Experience what it's like to have something positive happen. Let yourself receive this compliment. If some part of you thinks you didn't deserve it, try to see that as only a thought and focus on—and feel—the good in your body with your senses. Soak it in as much as possible. You deserve it.

4. If you've received a critique, again pause and feel your feet on the ground. Concentrate on what's happening in your body, rather than any reaction in your mind. If it feels uncomfortable, can you notice how that discomfort feels without automatically reacting?

5. As you focus on your body, remind yourself that this isn't personal. It's not about you. Take in what's helpful in the feedback and then come back to your body. Ask yourself, "What can I learn from this? Can any of this help me once I've calmed down a bit?"

6. Explore any judgments about yourself or the other person as just thoughts coming and going.

7. If someone criticizes you personally, acknowledge that it isn't a helpful critique, but a verbal slap. Feel that discomfort in your body without reacting to it. Explore the Dealing with Difficult People practice (page 109) to find a balanced response.

TAKE IT FURTHER

Sometimes, your brain needs to vent or share how it's reacting. There's a lot of momentum that comes up when you feel wronged. You don't have to ignore it. You can go for a run or write an angry letter, but don't send it—at least not until a day when you've cooled down to see if that's how you really want to respond.

Know Your Brain: Positive Neuroplasticity

With all the talk of stress and difficult emotions, it can seem like mindfulness focuses only on the negative. In fact, it's just as powerful to practice with the good stuff. Remember, the more your brain does a task, the stronger and more efficient the neural pathway for that task becomes. Whenever you notice contentedness, calm, peacefulness, delight, happiness, safety, comfort, or satisfaction, your brain gets better at recognizing them and making them a permanent fixture in your life.

Take time to focus on what you're good at, what you're capable of, and what you dream of doing. The more attention you pay to those moments, the more you'll notice them in the future. Every time you laugh with a friend, hear a good song, or eat something delicious, notice and savor those moments. Instead of focusing on how things could be different or what other people have that you don't, be mindful of what is working (you passed a test, assisted a goal, or helped a friend) and how you really are doing your best. Practice enjoying your achievements, even tiny ones like finishing a chapter in a book. You get to be in charge of growing your brain the way you want. Rather than thinking about meditation like medicine you take when you're sick, think of it like food that feeds your mind rather than your body.

CHAPTER SIX

Meditations for Self-Care

> *"It takes courage to grow up and become who you really are."*
>
> **E. E. CUMMINGS**

You get a million messages about the person you should be: what you're supposed to look like (big lips, flat abs, perfect eyebrows, and more); how you're supposed to act (tough, smart, funny, not too loud or quiet); and how you're supposed to express your sexual or gender identity. And somehow, amid all of that, you're also supposed to "be yourself." These practices are all about taking care of yourself just as you are. Then you can be in the best frame of mind to decide who you want to be.

Silencing Self-Criticism

Very few of us would talk to others the way we talk to ourselves. We'd never be so harsh or mean. Would you ever call your best friend the names you call yourself? Yet it seems to come naturally to be super self-critical.

Mindfulness helps you see that not only are those thoughts not true, they only have as much power as you give them. This practice lets you see your automatic thoughts without needing to believe them, and then choose a different response.

1. Take a moment to pause and notice what's going on right now. Use your senses to bring yourself into the present moment.

2. Notice any sensations in your body right now, particularly your feet on the floor. Remind yourself that it's okay to feel however you feel. Then keep coming back to the feeling of your breath and your feet. (You might also try the postures in the Self-Soothing Practices, page 50.)

3. Instead of focusing on the content of the thought, keep returning to how this moment feels in your body.

4. When you're ready, consider if there are any other ways of seeing this situation. Look for counterevidence. How would your best friend interpret this? How would you talk to your closest friend or family member if they were going through this?

5. Next, try to find a more balanced thought. Your automatic reaction might be, "I'm a loser. I always fail." A balanced response might be, "I made a mistake" or recognizing that you thought you'd fail last time but didn't.

6. The critical thought might not go away, but you don't need to fuel it. Remind yourself that the judgments in your head aren't true, no matter how convincing they are.

7. Keep your attention on your breathing and your body. You might choose to focus on something you're grateful for or even the tiniest thing that went well this week.

TAKE IT FURTHER

Almost everyone has this bully (or monster, demon, or troll) in their brain. However you picture it, it's very convincing, very persuasive, and quite charming. It tells you that it knows how to make you feel or be better, if only you'd listen to it. And it thrives on attention. The more you listen to it, the louder it gets. But here's the truth: It's wrong. It's totally wrong. You don't get better by making yourself feel worse. And while you might never be able to make it go away completely, if you know it's there, if you expect it, then it can't surprise you and knock you off balance as much. Use this practice to really see it. Even give it a name or decide what it looks like. Then the next time it shows up, it's not some immovable force. Instead, it's more like that smelly uncle at Thanksgiving. It's inevitably unpleasant, but you don't need to let it get to you.

Mindful Eating and Moving Mindfully

Have you ever eaten lunch and then forgotten that you did it? Ever walked home from school and didn't remember the walk at all? Or finished a bag of chips without even realizing you were eating? Most of us have had the experience of eating mindlessly or even going to the wrong place because we were distracted by something else. Mindfulness helps us be more present because we are attentive to what's happening as it's happening.

1. Whatever you are doing, take a moment to pause and set the intention to do it mindfully—just that one thing, right now.

2. Take a few deep breaths and notice how your body feels in this moment.

3. Then explore the task at hand with all of your senses.

4. If you're eating, notice what the food looks like, how the light hits it, how it smells, how it feels in your mouth as you chew and swallow. Really take your time with it. Put your fork down between bites. Notice any habits you might have, such as reaching for the next piece before finishing the first one. What is it like to just eat, rather than eating while looking at your phone or even listening to music?

CONTINUED

5. If you're walking, notice how your feet feel touching the ground. Hear any sounds that are around or within you. Try to place all of your attention on the feeling of walking. Notice how your muscles and joints propel you forward. It's actually amazing how much goes into keeping you upright and moving.

6. You can try this with any activity. Just use your senses to feel what's happening as it's happening. Whatever you are doing, try to do only that one thing.

7. When your mind wanders, bring your attention back to your senses in this moment.

AM I DOING THIS RIGHT?

This might feel weird at first. Who really pays attention to what walking or eating feels like? But the more you do it, the more you'll likely appreciate those chances to stop and just be. You don't even have to do it for the entire walk or meal. Try it with just a few bites or steps. See what happens when you commit to doing just one thing at a time.

Ever wake up and immediately feel like it's going to be a terrible day? Or you grab your phone before you're even fully awake? Those first few moments can help you set the tone for the rest of the day. This practice asks you to take just two minutes before picking up your phone or planning your day to be in your body and orient to your environment, so you can make a choice about how you're going to relate to yourself today.

1. You've just woken up. Notice how your body feels. Enjoy the feeling of not needing to do anything before your day starts. You might also check out the light in the room or the sounds you hear.

2. Take a few deep breaths. You can place your hands on your abdomen to feel your body breathing even more fully. Notice what it feels like to breathe.

3. Let your breathing be natural. Notice any stories or thoughts going through your mind. Send yourself kind thoughts (page 34) or set an intention for how you are going to be today. You might choose to be kind or compassionate or make someone else feel good. This isn't about ignoring anything negative; it's about choosing what you want to focus on.

CONTINUED

4. Take a few more moments to connect to your senses. Notice anything you can hear, smell, see, taste, or touch.

5. When you're ready or it's time to get up, renew your intention for how you want to be today. See if there's even one small thing you can look forward to or appreciate in this moment. Rest your attention on that kindness as you get up and go about your morning.

TAKE IT FURTHER

Each moment is an opportunity to start again. If you wake up feeling grouchy, let yourself feel that, name it, and notice that it moves and changes. Then come back to your body and to deciding how you want to be in this moment. You get to be in charge here.

It's important to know that this isn't about being super-optimistic or ignoring any problems you have. Rather, you're seeing that you get to decide, in every moment, how you are with whatever's happening. Consider how you really want to feel when you get back in bed at the end of the day.

Loving Your Body

Most of us have body-image issues, because we have this idea that our bodies don't look like they should. We believe we look wrong: wrong skin, height, legs, hair, everything. The amazing thing is that it doesn't matter what hair, skin, or height we have—someone will always say it should be different. It's like it is in elementary school, when no matter what your name is, someone will find a way to make fun of it. You can always choose to find something that isn't good enough.

Loving your body isn't about having the perfect arms, abs, or butt. And it doesn't mean you can't work out or eat healthy. It's about seeing that being kind to yourself makes you feel a lot better than treating yourself like crap and that you can choose which messages you take to heart.

1. Take a few deep breaths. Notice how you feel.

2. Let your breath be natural and turn your attention to what your body feels like.

3. Take some time to feel yourself breathing and try to marvel at the ability of your body to breathe and keep you alive.

CONTINUED

4. Notice that your senses are working all the time, giving you information and connecting you to the world. You don't even have to tell them to do anything; they just do it.

5. If you feel down or critical, take some time to notice how that feels inside. Let yourself feel that discomfort as sensations in your body rather than focusing on the thoughts or judgments themselves.

6. Try to avoid making major decisions right now. If your mind is saying, "I hate my body" or "I have the ugliest nose ever," try to notice that, right now, your mind is upset. Right now, you feel angry or sad. Right now, frustration feels this way. And it won't last forever even if it feels like it.

7. Remind yourself that you can't change your body by hating it. That only makes you feel worse. Remember that no one is perfect and pictures only tell part of a story. Imagine you could inhale peace and strength and exhale negativity and anger.

8. Take a few more deep breaths and notice how you feel now. Remind yourself that you are enough, just as you are. You might even say it in your head or out loud: "I am beautiful. I am enough. I am strong." Even if it feels strange or forced, the more you do this, the more you'll build kindness instead of judgment.

CHANGE IT UP

As you're noticing how you relate to your own body, notice if you're stuck in a pattern of checking out or critiquing other people. Observe how that makes you feel. You might try to send a silent compliment instead of a critique. Those kinder thoughts can actually have a very significant impact on your own mood and your relationship to others.

Making Choices about Technology

Did you know that tech companies deliberately make apps as addictive as possible? They spend billions of dollars researching ways to turn our phone use into a habit, something we can't live without even for five minutes. Some people call it "brain hacking." Phones aren't bad inherently, but they do become a problem when we check them without realizing it.

This meditation isn't about getting rid of the phone or social media. It's about recognizing how technology makes you feel and then deciding to use it only because you choose to, not because someone wants you to be addicted.

1. Pause. Take a few deep breaths. Notice how you feel as you breathe deeply.

2. Let your breathing be normal.

3. Take a moment to check in with how you feel as you go on social media or use your phone. What happens to your body and mind when you see someone else's photo or image of a perfect vacation? What thoughts automatically run through your mind? What happens in your body? Notice your jaw, your stomach, and your throat. What sensations can you feel?

4. As you notice how this feels, you might also ask yourself, "How does this post or picture make me feel?" Let the answer come to you.

5. As you keep looking or keep checking your feed, notice if you're always wanting more, comparing yourself, or perhaps telling yourself, "I'll be happy when I look like that . . . " Explore how these truly make you feel inside.

6. Let yourself be interested in this experience. It's not black and white. Observe all the nuances of what happens. Then you can decide how you want to proceed.

CHANGE IT UP

It seems ironic to suggest using an app to see how much you use other apps, but it can be really informative. Find an app that tracks your phone or social media use, and make the commitment to use it for three days. Notice what happens when you see the results. Did you know you were checking your phone that often? Then, you might try an experiment to you limit your phone use for a few days and see what happens. Notice how it feels. (Let your family and friends know what you're doing in advance, so they don't freak out.)

Taking Care of Yourself

Have you ever noticed that you can't focus when you're hungry? Or that your mood totally changes after you've gone for a walk or had a shower? How it's so much easier to get annoyed on an empty stomach? (That's why someone invented the word "hangry"!) It might seem rudimentary, but taking care of your own basic needs can change your mind-set, feelings, moods, emotions, and even levels of pain for an entire day. Use this practice as a way to check in with your basic needs before making judgments of yourself or your life.

1. If you find yourself starting to lose it, getting frustrated, wanting to run away, or getting really down on yourself, try to pause where you are and take a few deep breaths.

2. Let your breathing be natural and notice what you can feel with your senses. Feel your feet on the floor and the air on your skin. Notice what you hear and any tastes in your mouth.

3. Then check in with yourself. Before you judge yourself or give up, try to explore some of these questions:

    Have I eaten enough today?
    Have I drunk water in the last hour?

Could I use more sleep?
Have I gotten dressed today?
Have I showered?
Have I gone outside? Could I go for a walk?
Do I need a hug or connection with a friend?
Have I had any physical exercise at all today?

4. Whatever you need, make the decision to take care of yourself. If you can't do it right now, make a plan to do so when you are able. Remind yourself that whatever's going through your mind right now, you don't have to take it personally or give it too much focus. It's not you; it's hunger or fatigue or some other part of your system needing attention.

5. Once you tend to what you needed, notice how you feel. Take the time to really enjoy the shower or the glass of water. Explore how the air outside feels or what happens when you do put your phone down and take a nap.

TAKE IT FURTHER

Write yourself a reminder for what you need when you get down. Do you need to wait a few days after starting something new before you make a judgment of it? Do you need to go for a walk when you feel depressed? You might make a playlist of songs that bring your mood up when you need them. Then, next time you're feeling down, you have your own tailor-made prescription for what to do.

What to Do If You Feel Overwhelmed

There is nothing wrong with you if you feel like you can't meditate, you're losing it, or you can't think straight! Sometimes your nervous system overreacts or gets triggered, which makes you feel overwhelmed or out of control. Whether this happens while you're meditating or during the rest of your day, you can use these techniques to rebalance yourself. Find one or two that feel right to you.

BREATHE: It's annoying, but there's a reason everyone tells you to breathe when you're anxious. A deep breath is a signal to your nervous system that there aren't any threats around.

LONGER EXHALATION: This is the ultimate body hack. If you can lengthen your exhalation, you cue your nervous system to tell your body to chill out. It calls for the release of hormones that relax the whole system. Try to breathe in for a count of three or four and breathe out for a count of six to eight. Find the rhythm that works for you.

ASK YOURSELF: "What's the kindest thing I can do for myself right now? What do I need right now that will be helpful?" Focus on things that are healthy and nonaddictive, like going for a walk, resting, or exercising, rather than turning to something that might feel good in the short term but is actually harmful in the long term (like using technology or social media or mind-altering substances).

FOCUS ON OTHER PEOPLE: Sometimes the best thing you can do is to consider what kindness you could show for someone else right now. It's amazing how focusing on others' happiness gets us out of our own ruts. It doesn't have to be big. Write a note of kindness—saying *you're doing great* or *you got this*—and leave it on someone's locker or car. Give a random person a compliment. Even pick up a few pieces of garbage.

FOCUS ON THE MOST NEUTRAL THING IN YOUR BODY: This is usually your feet on the ground. Really put all of your energy and focus into feeling your feet. Notice how many toes you can feel without wiggling them. You might walk slowly to really emphasize the sensations.

FOCUS ON SOMETHING PLEASANT: Find a spot outside a window or in the sky that looks pleasing. Focus on a flower. Or notice the sound of the wind or the sun on your face. Let yourself really soak in those feelings and linger on what is pleasant to your system. See the Soaking in the Good practice (page 31).

ORIENT TO YOUR ENVIRONMENT: That means looking around you, specifically moving your head and neck to see in front, to the sides, and behind you. Notice anything that catches your eye.

If overwhelming feelings arise while meditating and you feel fine to keep going, try to be with the feelings for a bit and then come back out again, like dipping your toe in the water before swimming. Try the Self-Soothing Practices (page 50).

Conclusion

Being a teenager sucks a lot of the time. Making a commitment to mindfulness meditation won't get rid of the challenges of being a teenager, but it does mean you are choosing how you want those challenges to affect you.

The way to do this is to make mindfulness a regular part of your life. You brush your teeth every day because you know that's how you take care of them. You shower and change your clothes because you know you have to take care of your body. Isn't it bizarre that you do something every day for your teeth but not for your mind?

You don't need another person (or book) telling you what to do. If mindfulness becomes another chore you have to do or another thing you need to be good at, you'll probably never do it. The key to making this stick is to find out how it can work for you and with your life. It doesn't have to be big. The more you make it part of your regular routine, the easier it will be. And the more you actually enjoy it or make it fun, the more you'll keep doing it. Maybe you pick one of these practices to do each day. You might decide that taking a few breaths before and after school is enough. Or you might just find one or two things to be grateful for each day. Maybe you just mindfully listen to your favorite song or notice how you feel after you work out. Check it out for yourself and see what happens.

As you finish this book, you might take a moment for one final reflection:

1. Pause. Take a few deep breaths. Notice how you feel right now.

2. Let your breathing be natural. Check out what it's like to be you in this moment.

3. Explore how it feels to consider that every single person you meet is struggling with something. No one has it all figured out. That means it's totally normal for you to struggle or not know either. It means you can keep learning throughout your whole life.

4. As you feel your feet on the ground and your breath going in and out of your body, remind yourself that you are enough, just as you are. Even when it doesn't feel like it. Especially when it doesn't feel like it. You are enough. You are worthy. You're doing great.

5. Take a few more deep breaths. And remember that if you miss this moment, there's another one right . . . now.

Resources

Websites:

FOLLOWYOURBREATH.COM On my website, I offer mindfulness meditation classes, private coaching, and guided meditations.

IBME.COM Inward Bound Mindfulness Education is a nonprofit organization offering teen and adult mindfulness retreats.

JUSTMINDFULNESS.COM JusTme is a mindfulness instructor and mindful hip-hop artist working with K–12 students.

MBODIEDWISDOM.COM Embodied Wisdom provides education programs through individual and group coaching, online courses, mindfulness training, and retreats.

MINDFUL.ORG Mindful provides lots of articles, guided meditations, and resources to the mindfulness community.

MINDFULLIFEPROJECT.ORG Offers guided practices and free mindfulness hip-hop tracks.

CENTERFORMSC.ORG The Center for Mindful Self-Compassion shares tools, meditations, and insights on practicing self-compassion mindfully.

Books

ABBLETT, MITCH R., PHD, AND CHRISTOPHER WILLARD, PSYD. *Mindfulness for Teen Depression: A Workbook for Improving Your Mood.* Oakland, CA: Instant Help Books, 2016.

BLUTH, KAREN, PHD. *The Self-Compassion Workbook for Teens: Mindfulness and Compassion Skills to Overcome Self-Criticism and Embrace Who You Are.* Oakland, CA: Instant Help Books, 2017.

SEDLEY, BEN. *That Sucks: A Teen's Guide to Accepting What You Can't Change and Committing to What Your Can.* Oakland, CA: Instant Help Books, 2017.

SIEGEL, DANIEL. *Brainstorm: The Power and Purpose of the Teenage Brain.* New York: TarcherPerigree, 2014.

VO, DZUNG X., MD, FAAP. *The Mindful Teen: Powerful Skills to Help You Handle Stress One Moment at a Time.* Oakland, CA: Instant Help Books, 2015.

WILLARD, CHRISTOPHER, PSYD. *Mindfulness for Teen Anxiety: A Workbook for Overcoming Anxiety at Home, at School, and Everywhere Else.* Oakland, CA: Instant Help Books, 2014.

Other

BLAKEMORE, SARAH-JAYNE. "The Mysterious Workings of the Adolescent Brain." Filmed June 2012. TED video, 14:11. www.ted.com/talks/sarah_jayne_blakemore_the_mysterious _workings_of_the_adolescent_brain/transcript?language=en.

TEEN BREATHE MAGAZINE. www.breathemagazine.com /teen-breathe/

Apps

BREATHR: mindfulness app for youth; free for Android and Apple

HEADSPACE: one of the most popular meditation apps; subscription based (deals for students)

INSIGHT TIMER: lots of free guided meditations and meditation timer

MINDSHIFT: free app for teen anxiety

References

Allen, Summer. "The Science of Gratitude." Greater Good Science Center. May 2018. https://ggsc.berkeley.edu/images/uploads /GGSC-JTF_White_Paper-Gratitude-FINAL.pdf.

American Psychological Association. "Stress in America™ 2013 Highlights: Are Teens Adopting Adults' Stress Habits?" https://www.apa.org/news/press/releases/stress/2013/highlights.

Baijal, S., Jha, A. P., Kiyonaga, A., Singh, R., and Srinivasan, N. "The Influence of Concentrative Meditation Training on the Development of Attention Networks During Early Adolescence." *Frontiers in Psychology* 2 (2011): 1–9. doi:10.3389/fpsyg.2011.00153.

Barnes, V. A., Davis, H. C., Murzynowski, J. B., and Treiber, F. A. "Impact of Meditation on Resting and Ambulatory Blood Pressure and Heart Rate in Youth." *Psychosomatic Medicine* 66, no. 6 (2004): 909–914. doi:10.1097/01.psy.0000145902.91749.35.

Blakemore, S., and Choudhury, S. "Development of the Adolescent Brain: Implications for Executive Function and Social Cognition." *Journal of Child Psychology and Psychiatry* 47, no. 3-4 (2006): 296–312. doi:10.1111/j.1469-7610.2006.01611.x.

Bradt, Steve. "Wandering Mind Not a Happy Mind." *The Harvard Gazette.* November 11, 2010. https://news.harvard.edu/gazette /story/2010/11/wandering-mind-not-a-happy-mind/.

Burklund, L. J., Creswell, J. D., Irwin, M. R., and Lieberman, M. D. "The Common and Distinct Neural Bases of Affect Labeling and Reappraisal in Healthy Adults." *Frontiers in Psychology* 5, no. 221 (2014): doi:10.3389/fpsyg.2014.00221.

Carsley, D., Khoury, B., and Heath, N. L. "Effectiveness of Mindfulness Interventions for Mental Health in Schools: A Comprehensive Meta-Analysis." *Mindfulness* 9, no. 3 (2018): 693–707. doi: 10.1007 /s12671-017-0839-2.

Cooper, Anderson. "What Is 'Brain Hacking'? Tech Insiders on Why You Should Care." *CBS*. April 9, 2017. https://www.cbsnews.com /news/brain-hacking-tech-insiders-60-minutes/.

De Couck, M., Caers, R., Musch, L., Fliegauf, J., Giangreco, A., and Gidron, Y. "How Breathing Can Help You Make Better Decisions: Two Studies on the Effects of Breathing Patterns on Heart Rate Variability and Decision-Making in Business Cases." *International Journal of Psychophysiology* 139 (2019): 1–9. doi:10.1016 /j.ijpsycho.2019.02.011.

Emmons, R. A., and Mishra, A. "Why Gratitude Enhances Well-Being: What We Know, What We Need to Know." In K. M. Sheldon, T. B. Kashdan, and M. F. Steger, eds. *Series in Positive Psychology. Designing Positive Psychology: Taking Stock and Moving Forward.* New York: Oxford University Press (2011): 248–262.

Eponis | Sinope (blog). "Everything Is Awful and I'm Not Okay: Questions to Ask Before Giving Up." 2015. https://eponis.tumblr .com/post/113798088670/everything-is-awful-and-im-not-okay -questions-to.

Gottman, J., and Silver, J. *The Seven Principles for Making Marriage Work: A Practical Guide from the Country's Foremost Relationship Expert.* New York: Three Rivers Press, 1999.

Haase, L., Stewart, J. L., Youssef, B., May, A. C., Isakovic, S., Simmons, A. N., and Paulus, M. P. "When the Brain Does Not Adequately Feel the Body: Links Between Low Resilience and Interoception." *Biological Psychology* 113 (2016): 37–45. doi:.10.1016 /j.biopsycho.2015.11.004.

Himelstein, Sam. "Why Mindfulness Is a Good Skill for Teens to Learn." Center for Adolescent Studies. https://centerforadolescentstudies .com/why-mindfulness-is-a-good-skill-for-teens-to-learn/.

Hölzel, B. K., Carmody, J., Vangel, M., Congleton, C., Yerramsetti, S. M., Gard, T., and Lazar, S. W. "Mindfulness Practice Leads to Increases in Regional Brain Gray Matter Density." *Psychiatry Research: Neuroimaging* 191, no. 1 (2011): 36–43. doi:10.1016/j.pscychresns .2010.08.006.

Ireland, Tom. "What Does Mindfulness Meditation Do to Your Brain?" June 12, 2014. *Scientific American.* https://blogs.scientificamerican .com/guest-blog/what-does-mindfulness-meditation-do-to -your-brain/.

Korb, Alex. *The Upward Spiral: Using Neuroscience to Reverse the Course of Depression, One Small Change at a Time.* Oakland, CA: New Harbinger Publications, 2015.

Lin, C. C. "Gratitude and Depression in Young Adults: The Mediating Role of Self-Esteem and Well-Being." *Personality and Individual Differences* 87 (2015): 30–34. doi:10.1016/j.paid.2015.07.017.

Liu, Q. Q., Zhou, Z. K., Yang, X. J., Kong, F. C., Sun, X. J., and Fan, C. Y. "Mindfulness and Sleep Quality in Adolescents: Analysis of Rumination as a Mediator and Self-Control as a Moderator." *Personality and Individual Differences* 122 (2018): 171–176. doi:10.1016 /j.paid.2017.10.031.

Lyubomirsky, S. *The How of Happiness: A Scientific Approach to Getting the Life You Want.* New York: Penguin Press, 2007.

Meiklejohn, J., Phillips, C., Freedman, M. L., Griffin, M. L., Biegel, G., Roach, A., Frank, J., et al. "Integrating Mindfulness Training into K-12 Education: Fostering the Resilience of Teachers and Students." *Mindfulness* 3, no. 4 (2012): 291–307. doi:10.1007/s12671-012-0094-5.

Mrazek, M. D., Franklin, M. S., Phillips, D. T., Baird, B., and Schooler, J. W. "Mindfulness Training Improves Working Memory Capacity and GRE Performance while Reducing Mind Wandering." *Psychological Science* 24, no. 5 (2013): 776–781. doi:10.1177 /0956797612459659.

Napoli, M., Krech, P. R., and Holley, L. C. "Mindfulness Training for Elementary School Students: The Attention Academy." *Journal of Applied School Psychology* 21, no. 1 (2005): 99–125. doi:10.1300 /J370v21n01_05.

National Institute for the Clinical Application of Behavioral Medicine. Treating Trauma: 2 Ways to Help Clients Feel Safe, with Peter Levine. Streamed June 2, 2017. YouTube video, 6:33. https://www .youtube.com/watch?v=G7zAseaIyFA.

Neff, Kristen. "Self-Compassion." Accessed September 2019. https:// self-compassion.org/the-three-elements-of-self-compassion-2/.

Raes, F., Griffith, J. W., Van der Gucht, K., and Williams, J. M. G. "School-Based Prevention and Reduction of Depression in Adolescents: A Cluster-Randomized Controlled Trial of a Mindfulness Group Program." *Mindfulness* 5, no. 5 (2014): 477–486. doi:10.1007 /s12671-013-0202-1.

Sanger, K. L., and Dorjee, D. "Mindfulness Training for Adolescents: A Neurodevelopmental Perspective on Investigating Modifications in Attention and Emotion Regulation Using Event-Related Brain Potentials." *Cognitive, Affective, & Behavioral Neuroscience* 15, no. 3 (2015): 696–711. doi:10.3758/s13415-015-0354-7.

Schulte, Brigid. "Harvard Neuroscientist: Meditation Not Only Reduces Stress, Here's How It Changes Your Brain." *The Washington Post*. May 26, 2015. https://www.washingtonpost.com/news/inspired-life /wp/2015/05/26/harvard-neuroscientist-meditation-not-only

-reduces-stress-it-literally-changes-your-brain/?utm_term=
.fa40d13fba62.

Sibinga, E. M. S., Webb, L., Ghazarian, S. R., and Ellen, J. M. "School-Based Mindfulness Instruction: An RCT." *Pediatrics* 137, no. 1 (2016): 1–8. doi:10.1542/peds.2015-2532.

University of California, Los Angeles. "Putting Feelings into Words Produces Therapeutic Effects in the Brain." *ScienceDaily.* June 22, 2007. www.sciencedaily.com/releases/2007/06/070622090727.htm.

University of Cambridge. "Mindfulness Meditation Increases Well-Being in Adolescent Boys, Study Finds." *ScienceDaily.* September 1, 2010. www.sciencedaily.com/releases/2010/09/100901111720.htm.

Watkins, P. C., Woodward, K., Stone, T., and Kolts, R. L. "Gratitude and Happiness: Development of a Measure of Gratitude and Relationships with Subjective Well-Being." *Social Behavior and Personality* 31, no. 5 (2003): 431–452. doi:10.2224/sbp.2003.31.5.431.

Wisner, B. L., Jones, B., and Gwin, D. "School-Based Meditation Practices for Adolescents: A Resource for Strengthening Self-Regulation, Emotional Coping, and Self-Esteem." *Children & Schools* 32, no. 3 (2010): 150–159. doi:10.1093/cs/32.3.150.

Young, Shinzen. "A Pain-Processing Algorithm." Last modified December 7, 2016. https://www.shinzen.org/wp-content/uploads/2016/12/art_painprocessingalg.pdf.

Zenner, C., Herrnleben-Kurz, S., and Walach, H. "Mindfulness-Based Interventions in Schools—A Systematic Review and Meta-Analysis." *Frontiers in Psychology* 5 (2014). doi:10.3389/fpsyg.2014.00603.

Acknowledgments

It's an honor to express my gratitude to some of the people who've helped me along the way.

To Alan Brown, my partner and friend, who lets me edit out all of his words and makes me a better teacher. Even if I could do this without you, it would never be as sassy, as intuitive, or as much fun.

Special thanks to Argos Gonzalez for your support and for being a true friend, and to Devon Cresci for your insight and inspiration.

There is no teacher without students. Over the years, I have learned far more from my students than I have taught. Thank you for letting me lead with love.

To Aria, my BBG. For being my best mindfulness teacher, reminding me to breathe when I need it, and for all the moments of emergency coolness. You inspire me to be the best version of myself.

To my parents and brothers for putting up with me as a teenager and beyond.

Finally, to Cam. For reading every draft, editing every doc, and supporting my every step. For all this and more. I love you with everything I have.

DR. NICOLE LIBIN, Ph.D. is a certified mindfulness educator and facilitator and an adjunct professor. She has designed and facilitated mindfulness curricula and other courses for Mindful Schools, Mount Royal University, and numerous private organizations and has taught mindfulness to adults, adolescents, children, and anyone else who will let her stop and take a breath with them.

She has written two other books on mindfulness. *Sticky Brains* is a mindfulness and brain science picture book for children. Her other book, *Mindful Parenting Practices for a Chaotic World,* offers real-world mindfulness tools for busy parents.

Nicole lives in Calgary, Canada, with her husband, Cam, and her daughter, Aria (who continues to be her best mindfulness teacher and the greatest weighted blanket of all time).

For more information, including guided meditations and more practice suggestions, see followyourbreath.com.

9 781641 528375